FROM
DESPAIR
TO
Delight

A TRUE STORY
of GOD'S FAITHFULNESS *to* CHANGE
A LIFE FOREVER *and* ALWAYS

FROM
DESPAIR
TO
Delight

A TRUE STORY
of GOD'S FAITHFULNESS to CHANGE
A LIFE FOREVER and ALWAYS

PAT FREEMAN

NEW YORK

FROM DESPAIR TO *Delight*

By Pat Freeman

ISBN: 978-1-60037-486-9 **Paperback**

Published by:

MORGAN · JAMES
THE ENTREPRENEURIAL PUBLISHER™

Morgan James Publishing, LLC
1225 Franklin Ave Ste 325
Garden City, NY 11530-1693
Toll Free 800-485-4943
www.MorganJamesPublishing.com

Cover Wrap & Interior Design & Layout by:
Heather Kirk
www.GraphicsByHeather.com
Heather@GraphicsByHeather.com

Habitat for Humanity®
Peninsula
Building Partner

Isaiah 40:26

Lift up your eyes on high
And see who has created these stars,
The One who leads forth their host by number,
He calls them all by name;
Because of the greatness of
His might and the strength
Of His power
Not one of them is missing.

Dedicated to

Lois, my Titus Woman, (Titus 2:3–5) whose
faithful teaching of the Word of God, with a meek
and gentle spirit, gave me a firm foundation, and
Matt, a friend who walked many paths by my side,
prayed for me, and always listens to my heart.

ACKNOWLEDGEMENTS

The writing of my first book has taught me a valuable lesson, that is, I could not accomplish this alone. Even in the beginning, before many knew I was writing, the Lord was with me, and there were a few praying for me. Many thanks need to be given for this finished work.

First, I give thanks to the Lord, whose presence, guidance, and direction gave birth to this book. I believe it was His will that this book was published. Second, I give thanks for each person He placed in my life, because without their involvement, I could not have completed it.

In the beginning God used Carol DeRoy to plant the seed, and then Carol, Robin Belanger, Karen Coyle, Fiona Dietzel, Donna Thomas, Helena Klausen, and Beth Ann Wiersma (who has been my faithful prayer partner for two years), prayed faithfully. They also faithfully supported me with much encouragement as the writing progressed. Carol also read some of my rough draft, and helped me in those places where I had forgotten some of my English grammar.

When the writing was finished, the publication process began, and thanks must go to those who supported me in this also. I owe a debt of gratitude to Ben and Tiffany vanKlinken, Jay and Alison vanKlinken, Jim and Karen Coyle, Mark Beauchamp, Shirley Morden, my friend for many years, and Maryka Vandescheur, who were invaluable to me.

Praise goes to my son Scott who read my work, encouraged me, and helped me with the computer. He has tried patiently to teach me Word 2007.

Words of thanks hardly seem enough for Beth Ann, who generously, and willingly "no thanks are needed" she said, agreed to edit this manuscript. She has worked tirelessly and for many hours correcting this first-time author's work. I have thanked God many times for her in my life. With the editing finished, proof readers were needed, and again God provided. Much time was given by Jim and Karen, Cindy Dennis, Alison, Helena, Shirley, Beth Ann, and Kingsley Archer to proof read the work to pick up any of my errors in the editing process. I am grateful to all of them.

I also want to thank Rose Oosterhof who has contributed to the cover design. She stepped forward and volunteered to help as soon as she was aware of the need.

Finally, I wish to thank all those at Morgan James Publishing who have guided this stumbling author through the process to bring my manuscript to publication. I thank Margo Toulouse especially for her patience in answering unending questions and listening to me through many, many emails. At the end of this long list for thanks are the family members who have cared for me and supported me.

No one knows at this time all of God's purpose in this project, but I can only hope that everyone involved in getting this work published would be able to know my deep heartfelt appreciation for their effort and dedication.

CONTENTS

INTRODUCTION

Reading can be a wonderful pastime. There is a whole world out there between the pages of a book. I have traveled through some of the world's greatest cities, sailed across its oceans, lived intrigue, romance, and laughter through the pages of the books I have devoured over the years. Yet, until now, the thought of being the author of one never occurred to me.

Have you had the experience of the Lord urging you to do something you have never attempted before? It is not only frightening but also exciting. It brings to my mind the scene of a father in the water and the child on the dock, and the father is saying, "Its okay. Don't be afraid to jump; I'll catch you."

Feeling the same trepidation that child would feel, I have come to the computer to write this book. It covers the years from 1972 to the present. It is meant to keep your focus on what God did, and is doing, and how He worked through those years to change me, bringing me from the depths of despair, to the place of learning to delight myself in Him. Psalm 37:4, "Delight yourself in the Lord; And He will give you the desires of your heart."

Briefly, I will explain how writing this book came about. I was teaching a ladies' evening Bible study group in my home. It was an extension of our Ministry of Women at the church. In my teaching, I was using many examples from my own experience. One particular evening I was sharing about the place of despair I was in that had brought me to the Lord and how much God had changed me. I used the phrase, "from despair to delight." One of the ladies smiled at me and said, "You should write a book!" I laughed and replied, "Sounds like a plan, I will call it, *From Despair to Delight.* Everyone laughed along with me. But the Lord planted a seed that night. The idea nagged at me, and brought me to the place where I began to pray about it. I then asked two ladies close to me to pray about it with me.

As I share my life in this book, I trust that I can leave you with the sense of how blessed I am, even though I have walked some difficult paths. The apostle Paul left us with his wonderful confidence in God in his letter to the Romans, "And we know that God causes all things to work together for good to those who love God, to those who are called according to His purpose" (8:28). David also learned this valuable truth, that God has a plan for our lives: "Your eyes have seen my unformed substance; And in Your book were all written The days that were ordained for me, When as yet there was not one of them" (Psalm 139:16). That God had his life all planned out, and written down before he was even born, was very real to David. Paul and David both understood that God was in control of the events of their lives.

The following is the story of my journey through the "**ALL**" things in my life that God worked out for my good, and also how He fit me into His plan that had been written down in His Book long before this life began for me. God is so faithful, and I am so thankful that He unfolded His plan day by day and did not let me see the future. This has not been an easy book to write, and for some of you, it will not be an easy read, but I hope it will be an encouragement to you to "live one day at a time" for His glory.

At the beginning of this process, I had a hard time believing God really wanted me to do this, but I just kept on praying, and day by day,

I kept working at it. This book is the result. May God take it and use it for His glory, and I pray that as you read it, you will be blessed and encouraged to wholly trust our God, and that you might learn to truly delight yourself in the Lord.

ONE

A New Dawn

Getting up early in the morning has always been a passion of mine. There is serenity and peaceful quiet in the hours before the sun gets up, while the world is still asleep. The uniqueness of each season lends its beauty to the surroundings as dawn breaks. In the spring, it's the cool air coming in the bedroom window that greets me, with the birds chirping and chattering to each other. Above all the other sounds, I can hear the call of the morning dove. In summer, the light comes earlier, and the air is warmer. These are the mornings I can take my coffee, sit out on the patio, enjoy the quietness and read. The autumn brings back cooler air and with it vibrant colors. It's amazing to me how every fall I am awed by the colors in the trees as if I had never seen them before. And then there is my favourite, the winter mornings.

It seems like many people do not like the winter. In Canada, our snow-birds (seniors) fly south for the winter just as our Canada geese do. But I could not bear the thought of missing the beauty of winter. Even in winter, I love to have my bedroom window open to the cold air when I sleep. Everything feels crisp and fresh. When I awake on winter mornings and there has been a fresh blanket of snow overnight, it looks as if God has thrown down a covering of twinkling jewels while I slept. How I thank God that I have been blessed to live in a region with four distinctive seasons.

There are many of us who are born in a certain area and live there all our lives, without the necessity, or opportunity, to move. I am one of those people. I have always lived within an hour's radius of my birthplace. Living in Southwestern Ontario, in Canada, has been a rare gift in a life that has had "deep valleys," as well as some "mountaintop" experiences.

Going back and rehearsing all the sin and failure or the years before I had Christ in my life is not the purpose here, so I will try to condense that time for you. I was brought up in a home with an alcoholic father that didn't want me. He never wanted to be with me, nor did he ever show me any physical kind of affection. It was difficult living with the poverty his drinking brought to our home, and only caused a strong desire in me to get away from it. Getting pregnant at sixteen forced me into a marriage that turned out to be loveless and empty. I found myself with an angry, drinking husband, six children I didn't think I wanted, and anger and frustration over where I had ended up. I was in a place of total despair.

Both my mother and my uncle were Christians, so I had heard the gospel from an early age. My mom always made sure, wherever we were living, that we went to Sunday school. However, I was rebellious and refused to listen. I am so thankful that God heard my family's prayers on my behalf. I don't know exactly how they worded them, but I only know that God worked: one day I would be on my knees crying out to Him in desperation. I remember asking Him to help me because I couldn't get through another day of living without hope. I've discovered that hopelessness can be a blessing when it drives you to your knees. David writes in Psalm 119:71 "It is good for me that I was afflicted, That I may learn Your statutes." And I did learn.

By 1972 both my parents had died. My dad had passed away in 1967, and my mom in 1969. My only sibling, my sister, had been living in Calgary for 20 years, and we were not very close. My husband Tom and I had been separated for about nine months, and I had come back to our home to try again to make something out of our marriage. It wasn't working. I felt so lost and alone.

Then one Saturday morning, a young man from Temple Baptist Church, out visiting homes in our area, came to our door. He told me that he had been talking to my children about coming to Sunday school on the bus. Thank God they wanted to go. I asked my husband if it would be alright, and he said he didn't care. This was to be the beginning of the miraculous way God would work out His plan for me.

Eleven years before, in 1961, I had gone to Temple Baptist Church for a brief time, walked the aisle, asked Christ to save me, and was baptized. The problem was, at that time, I did not have any idea about how to live as a Christian, and Tom and his family were against me going to church.

During that same time I also had no understanding of trusting Jesus for His power or how to live to please Him. I eventually stopped trying and quit going to church. It does not take long for one to grow cold to spiritual things when one stops assembling with believers. Hebrews 10:25 says, "not forsaking our own assembling together, as is the habit of some, but encouraging one another; and all the more as you see the day drawing near."

So in 1972 the children and I started attending Temple, and every week we would get on the bus for Sunday school and church. It was still a struggle. I knew the teaching I was receiving at Temple Baptist Church was the truth and what I was looking for, but how to appropriate these truths to my life was something I couldn't seem to understand. I kept asking God to give me the understanding that I needed. I longed desperately to please God, but I was still miserable at home. I was sharing this with a Christian friend, and she suggested I read *The Greatest is Love* (1967, A Paraphrased New Testament).

It was the living New Testament. I think I read it from cover to cover in three days. I couldn't put it down. Like the man in the Gospel of John who was blind, but was healed and saw (9:25), so the Holy Spirit opened my understanding to the Scriptures and started a fire in my heart, which thank God, still burns as bright today as it did then. I was alive. Everything was new. I couldn't stop reading the Bible, and I couldn't stop talking about it. God had faithfully answered my prayers and made Christ real to me through the Scriptures.

My perspective was brand new. It was as if the sun was brighter and the grass was greener, and I began to see things differently. Very quickly I had changed, and my poor husband was married to a stranger. He knew how to deal with me in my anger, my complaining, and my rages, but what in the world would he do with the changed me? I suppose he did the only thing he could think of, and that was to be with me as little as possible. Our failing relationship had just gotten worse.

Tom had begun bowling about 10 years before, but now he was gone constantly. I don't want anyone to think that I totally changed overnight in every way, but I had become a new creature in Christ. "Therefore if anyone is in Christ, he is a new creature" (2 Corinthians 5:17), and there was a newness to my thinking. I started to see how God valued my husband and children, and my feelings about my family were changing.

It would have been wonderful if everything in every area of my life had changed instantly; however, like everyone, this being made into the image of Christ is a process, and it takes time. It takes time to learn and time to grow up in our faith, just as it takes time to grow up from a child into an adult. 1 Peter 2:2 says, "Like newborn babies, long for the pure milk of the word, so that by it you may grow in respect to salvation." I was learning that I needed to do some growing up spiritually.

As I began to see how wrong I was in my attitudes and behavior regarding my relationship to my husband, I would apologize to him for being angry or sarcastic in my responses. He was very uncomfortable with that. Instead of the change in me making him interested in becoming a Christian, all it seemed to do was make him more angry and belligerent with me. One day I was telling him how sorry I was for getting angry with him, and had asked him to forgive me again, when he began to shake me. He said, "If you say you are sorry one more time, I'm going to strangle you." I had never really given any thought to apologies before, so Tom was hard-pressed to understand this change in me. It was a very frightening experience for me, yet even at this time, God gave me the ability to have compassion on Tom, so I understood the struggle he had coping with the new me.

God began to show me that the foremost relationship in my life was with Him, followed closely by my relationship with my husband. I want to give you a snapshot of Tom, so you can understand why I was the one who needed to learn how to love him with God's unconditional love, and how much I needed Biblical teaching.

Tom was born into a family that never understood how to show feelings, or express love. He had one younger brother, and an absentee father much of the time. His dad worked out of town for most of Tom's life and only came home on his days off. Tom's dad was the type of guy who catered to his mother because it was easier than causing any ripples. Tom's mother was not a nurturing woman, so he spent most of his growing up years with his maternal grandparents, and because he was favored and doted on as a child, he grew up very spoiled.

He met me, in 1953, when he was 17 years old, and he was already drinking, had quit school, and spent most of his free time at the billiards hall. I look back and ask myself, "what was I thinking?" but it is obvious that I wasn't. I can see now that he could not possibly know anything about marriage, or loving a wife or family, but at 14 years old, I was swept up by his good looks, his father's new car, the fact that this guy would find me attractive, and also by my own immaturity. I also understand now that I just wanted to be loved, and I was asking something from Tom that he was unable to give me. We were a disaster waiting to happen, but God had other plans. The Scriptures have some wonderful statements and promises, and some of the best are the "But God's."

The Apostle Paul tells us in Ephesians 2:1–3 who and where we are without Christ, and then he begins with a "But God" to tell us what God has done for us in Christ. "But God, being rich in mercy, because of His great love with which He loved us, even when we were dead in our transgressions, made us alive together with Christ (by grace you have been saved), (Ephesians 2:4–5). So even though Tom and I seemed headed for disaster, God knew the plans He had for our lives in the future. We ended up married in 1956 when I was three months pregnant. That was just the beginning of the difficult years ahead which God would use to bring me to Himself. The more I come to know Him, the more I can truly thank Him for that time.

Spending daily time in prayer and asking God to save Tom became a priority. It was a matter of just believing God that it would happen. The Scriptures say that anything we ask in Jesus name, believing, He will do it (John 14:14). I now had that truth to cling to. I simply wanted to learn how to live so that my life would impact my family. God was faithful and answered my prayers, but never in a million years would I have imagined how He was going to do that.

A wonderful gift from the Lord came to me, in the form of a person with a great gift for teaching and mentoring. Titus 2:3–5 tells us how to live as mature women believers:

> *Older women likewise are to be reverent in their behavior, not malicious gossips nor enslaved to much wine, teaching what is good, so that they may encourage the young women to love their husbands, to love their children, to be sensible, pure, workers at home, kind, being subject to their own husbands, so that the word of God will not be dishonored.*

She did that faithfully. I was like an explorer, embarking on a journey that would take me to places I had never been before. It would be exciting, but difficult, and sometimes so painful; without Christ I could not have made it through. Come; meet Lois.

TWO
Lois

By 1973, I had begun to form some friendships at Temple Baptist church. Seventeen years of marriage had been a continuous struggle for both of us. There was no sense of oneness or belonging to each other in our relationship, but I was beginning to find a sense of belonging at the church. It was at this time that Jean (one of the ladies at the church), and I became friends, and through Jean, God directed me to Lois. Jean so openly displayed a close relationship to Christ that I began to ask her about this relationship. I knew Jean had something that I did not understand. She had such peace and joy, even though she also had a husband that was not a Christian.

As Jean began to share with me the things she was learning, I was amazed because I had never heard of "The Abundant Life in Christ" before. This teaching, of abundant living was taken from Scripture, and was part of the lessons that Lois was teaching. This was based on John 10:10 that says, "The thief comes only to steal and kill and destroy; I came that they may have life, and have it abundantly." As Jean and I talked, a hunger began to grow in me to know more about abundant living, and I longed for the kind of teaching Jean was getting. This longing led to my introduction to Lois, and thus, the beginning of my discipleship with her.

The discipleship program that Jean was involved in was a weekly meeting with Lois in her home. Lois was teaching lessons that she had designed based on *"Ten Steps to Christian Maturity"* compiled by Campus Crusade for Christ. Jean explained that Lois broke all the chapters down into smaller lessons and added a lot of Scripture memorization. Jean knew that Lois had learned through her own experiences that smaller amounts of the Word of God, committed to memory, had truly blessed her life more than trying to read many chapters, but not remembering what she had read.

At the time Jean told me all about her Bible study, Lois would have been in her early fifties, so Jean and I would have been considered the young women that the Bible describes as needing to be taught all about loving our husbands and children (Titus 2:3–5). I was in my early thirties when all this happened. I really thought I was young at the time, but later wished I had learned many of these truths much sooner. Thinking of Jean and what she was learning caused me to pick up the phone and call Lois.

Lois was gracious. From the first phone call, to actually meeting her, her graciousness was what stood out. In 1 Peter 3, Peter is speaking to wives about Godly living. In verse 4 he says, "but let it be the hidden person of the heart, with the imperishable quality of a gentle and quiet spirit, which is precious in the sight of God." That very aptly described Lois.

Now, you need to know that I am a sanguine. This is that type of personality (when it is not controlled by the Holy Spirit) enters the room mouth first. A sanguine is a loud, boisterous, kind of "bull in a china shop" person. I have a deep, belly laugh that you can hear upstairs, downstairs, and all around the house. If you understand the character of the apostle Peter before he was changed, you have met me. So, you can imagine how I felt when I met Lois. Oh how I wanted to be just like her, sweet, gracious, and gentle in spirit. I praise the Lord who, over the years, has changed me into a completely different person than I was before I was saved, but I'm still not done working on the gentle and quiet spirit area.

Thank God, Lois said yes, she would do the discipleship program with me. It makes sense that she started at the very beginning with me. "How do you feel about the Word of God?" she asked me the first day. "I believe it," I said. This was the foundation to all I would learn. Isaiah 55:10-11 says,

> For as the rain and the snow come down from heaven, And do not return there without watering the earth And making it bear and sprout, And furnishing seed to the sower and bread to the eater; So will My word be which goes forth from My mouth; It will not return to Me empty, Without accomplishing what I desire, And without succeeding in the matter for which I sent it.

Here we see that the rain and snow have a definite purpose for which God has designed them. So it is with His Word. 1 Peter 1:25 says, "BUT THE WORD OF THE LORD ENDURES FOREVER." And this is the word which was preached to you."

Lois immediately realized that I needed to examine my attitude to the Word of God. We must believe all of the Word and understand you can't just pick and choose out of it what you want to believe. Truth is truth. We can accept it or reject it, but that won't change it. It makes me think of gravity. You can't see it, but if you don't believe it, and jump off a ten-story building, you will be certain to find out it exists, and that the teaching of the Law of Gravity is truth.

Lois and I began meeting weekly. I was starting from scratch, and dealing with an enormous amount of insecurity. Both of the major male influences in my life, my father and my husband, gave me no sense of either love or security. Now, I was supposed to put all my security in a male figure, my heavenly Father. I knew I was born again, a child of God, but my personal knowledge of Him, and the security He could provide was sketchy.

Lois began to teach me to pray specific prayers that went along with the Scriptures she was teaching me. The two main prayers were, "Father, please give me the love I need for Tom, because I can't love him in my own strength," and "Father, make my security in you real to me." I needed to see Tom through God's eyes, with His love and compassion, just as God had seen me. There was no way I could humanly do this. By the time God had got a hold on my life, I hated Tom, and I just wanted him gone out of my life. But at the same time, I wanted change that came with living for my Savior. Remember, I wanted what Jean had. Thus began the daily, nitty-gritty work of choosing obedience to God over my feelings and bad habits.

1 John 5:14-15 says:

> *This is the confidence which we have before Him, that, if we ask anything according to His will, He hears us. And if we know that He hears us in whatever we ask, we know that we have the requests which we have asked from Him.*

So, in praying these prayers, I was certain that God heard me and would answer. I began to see Tom differently. I began to have such a longing in my heart for him to know the Lord personally. I wanted to do things for him. Now, don't get me wrong; this wasn't easy, and it didn't happen overnight. I got so that I knew 1 John 1:9, "If we confess our sins, He is faithful and righteous to forgive us our sins and to cleanse us from all unrighteousness." better than any other verse in the Bible. I had to ask forgiveness so many times, I had that verse memorized.

Discouragement was a big problem for me. It seemed that no matter how much effort I put into practicing what I was learning, it did not make any difference with Tom. I wanted to give up, and sometimes I would for days on end. I would wallow in my frustration and anger. But God never quit showing me how much He loved me, and that He loved Tom the same way.

Many of us as new Christians have a struggle with remembering where we came from. It doesn't take long for the devil to deceive us into self-righteousness, and we begin to think that God doesn't like the unsaved person. It's as if we are better than everyone else because we're living for the Lord. Well, guess what? I've been there, and it didn't take long for God to show me otherwise.

After the initial week of finding out what my attitude needed to be toward the Bible, Lois presented me with five Scripture verses. She told me that if I never had the opportunity to learn more, I could have an abundant life based on the truth in these verses.

They were;

1. Isaiah 41:10: *"Do not fear, for I am with you; do not anxiously look about you, for I am your God. I will strengthen you, surely I will help you, Surely I will uphold you with My righteous right hand."*

2.   Philippians 4:13: *"I can do all things through Him who strengthens me."*

3.   Philippians 4:19: *"And my God will supply all your needs according to His riches in glory in Christ Jesus."*

4.   1 Corinthians 10:13: *"No temptation has overtaken you but such as is common to man; and God is faithful, who will not allow you to be tempted beyond what you are able, but with the temptation will provide the way of escape also, so that you will be able to endure it."*

5.   Romans 8:28–29: *"And we know that God causes all things to work together for good to those who love God, to those who are called according to His purpose. For those whom He foreknew, He also predestined to become conformed to the image of His Son, so that He would be the firstborn among many brethren;"*

The first one (Isaiah 41:10) would turn out to be my life verse. Many times when I struggled with feeling overwhelmed with my circumstances, I would pray and ask God for strength from His Word, and this verse would quickly come to mind. Sometimes I felt like I was hanging on to it for dear life. God has promised us to be our strength and help so we have no need to fear or be upset. Philippians 4:13 promises that we can do everything He asks of us, being obedient to His Word, through Jesus Christ's own power and strength. God also says, Philippians 4:19, He will take care of every need through His incredible resources in Jesus.

The daily temptation into sin faced by all believers is also taken care of by the truth that God will not allow a temptation beyond what can be handled (1 Corinthians 10:13). It need not overpower the believer.

God is faithful. In her book, *Having a Mary's Spirit*, Johanna Weaver shares a story about a young mother. She prayed that God would show her the way out of her problem with drinking with her co-workers on payday while picking up her paycheck. He did that through her young son, who constantly requested to go with her. She did not want him to see her drinking, so she had always refused him. God showed her that having her son with her gave her the reason she needed to not stay and drink on payday (2006, p. 188). I prayed to God to show me the way out of my TV habit, because TV had become my place of escape from the reality of my circumstances. God began to show me that I could be changed by learning to apply His Word to my life.

The fifth Scripture Lois gave me at the beginning in 1973 was the very familiar Romans 8:28-29. I have met many believers who say they believe the Bible, yet don't accept the truth of this Scripture. I am firmly convinced that in the life of His child, God is in control. God's purpose is to make us into the image of His Son. Whatever comes into our lives, whether it's through trials, blessings, good or bad, God is at work in us, using our minutes, our hours, and our days to make us like Jesus.

These portions of Scripture have had a profound impact on my life. I can think of only one word to describe what God had started, "Wow." Lois continued to faithfully teach me the Word of God week by week. We did not take major breaks, stopping only for two week summer vacations, and taking off a few days at Christmastime. The topics such as love, anger, an unequally yoked marriage, trusting, discipline, and abiding in Christ, were looked at, and discussed from a Biblical standpoint. What did the Word of God have to say? What was God's perspective on the subject? She always stayed faithful to the Word of God. She had such love and courage to speak the truth even when it was hard, and I didn't want to hear it.

Some Scriptures brought such conviction that I wanted to tear some of the pages out of my Bible. I wanted to deal with Tom out of my old sin nature, giving in to anger and frustration, when my emotions clashed with Scriptural truth. I struggled with those feelings many times as Lois presented lessons to me, but her patient, gentle spirit would win me over. She would take me to the portions of Scripture that encouraged me, like Philippians 1:6, "For I am confident of this very thing, that He who began a good work in you will perfect it until the day of Christ Jesus." Lois reminded me that God would never give up on me, and that He wanted to change me. I have thanked God for her many, many times.

Sometimes I was so discouraged, I wanted to give up. Discouragement became a constant companion to me, snapping at my heels, trying to trip me up. I can still hear Lois' quiet voice telling me over and over that discouragement is of the devil. If he can get you to quit, you give him the victory, and that is exactly what he wants you to do. I cried a river of tears. I felt I could relate to Jeremiah:

> *You who know, O Lord, Remember me, take notice of me,*
> *And take vengeance for me on my persecutors. Do not, in view*
> *of Your patience, take me away; Know that for Your sake I*
> *endure reproach. Your words were found and I ate them, and*
> *Your words became for me a joy and the delight of my heart;*
> *For I have been called by Your name, O Lord God of hosts. I*
> *did not sit in the circle of merrymakers, Nor did I exult.*
> *Because of Your hand upon me I sat alone, For You filled me*
> *with indignation. Why has my pain been perpetual And my*
> *wound incurable, refusing to be healed? Will You indeed be*
> *to me like a deceptive stream With water that is unreliable?*
> *Therefore, thus says the Lord, "If you return, then I will*

restore you— Before Me you will stand; And if you extract the precious from the worthless, You will become My spokesman. They for their part may turn to you, But as for you, you must not turn to them." (Jeremiah 15:15–19)

Jeremiah was being used as an object lesson and it was hard. Not one person in Israel accepted or wanted his message. He was barely able to keep from letting discouragement overcome him. That is exactly how I felt in my own home. How much easier it would have been to just go along with Tom and our children, making choices that pleased them rather than choosing to please God. Jeremiah did not quit, and praise God, neither did I.

Out of necessity, I pushed on and persisted with studying, and slowly I began to see change. My excitement about what God was doing began to grow. I cannot record all of my experiences which God used to cause me to grow through this time under Lois' teaching, so I will share one that made a significant impact on me and stands out in my mind.

One that stands out clearly was the day that God used me to lead someone to Him for the first time. Cheryl was my daughter Nancy's friend from high school, whom I had not seen for quite a while because she had gone away to university. Once in a while she would pop in, say hello and off she would go again. It was just an ordinary morning when there was a knock at the door, and there was Cheryl.

"Come in and sit down," I greeted her. "Nancy isn't home."

"I didn't come to see Nancy; I came to see you," she said.

Cheryl had come to ask me if I would do Bible study with her. "You're the only one I know that knows the Bible," she remarked.

To say that I was surprised would be an understatement. She had never shown any interest in spiritual things any time that I was around her, but apparently she had been studying with the Jehovah's Witnesses and was very confused. I told her I would be glad to study with her and arranged to meet with her in a couple of days. I was very nervous about doing this as I had never taught the Bible to an unbeliever before, so I immediately called Lois. She gave me some advice and told me to start by sharing a salvation tract, *The Four Spiritual Laws*.

The tract presents the Gospel of salvation very clearly. It has very specific graphics that show the great chasm that exists between us and God, and how our sin has cut us off from fellowship with Him. Then it gives all the Scripture references to the death, burial and resurrection of Christ. It is a wonderful tool to use for anyone to present the Gospel to an unbeliever.

Cheryl came back at our arranged meeting time. I had asked Lois to pray, and I had also spent much time in prayer since Cheryl had left, and now trusting the Lord, I shared my tract with her. I simply pointed out the great gulf between her and God because of her sin, and how God had provided all she needed in Jesus to come into a right relationship with Him. I expected some argument, but when I asked her if she wanted to pray and repent of her sin and receive Christ, she very quietly, with tears running down her face, said "yes." It was all done very simply and quietly. She prayed, and I prayed.

Satan has tried so many times to convince me that nothing happened that day, but Cheryl's life is a living testimony of how God saves, changes and uses people. Cheryl did Bible study with me for two years. She also went to Lois for mentoring, and then attended London Baptist Bible College and Seminary. There, God put a burden on her heart for missions, and she met the man who would be her husband at a missionary conference. They spent a number of years ministering in Pakistan and are now serving in Kazakhstan.

There is such unbelievable joy in being used by the Lord. Imagine, being used by the "God of Moses" to further His Kingdom. Being the vessel used by God to lead Cheryl to Christ, and to know the impact she has had on the Kingdom of God, has been a highlight of my Christian life. I believe that the teaching I was receiving from Lois was the reason God could use me in Cheryl's life.

The opportunity to spend that time under Lois' teaching has made all the difference in my Christian walk. "but speaking the truth in love, we are to grow up in all aspects into Him who is the head, even Christ," Ephesians 4:15. Lois in her gentle way did this. Her faithfulness to the Word of God, has meant much to me over the years, and continues to do so today as I continue to teach what she taught me. Lois was a special gift to me from God.

We are exhorted over and over again in the Scriptures to study the Word of God. The Apostle Paul writes to Timothy, "Be diligent to present yourself approved to God as a workman who does not need to be ashamed, accurately handling the word of truth" (2 Timothy 2:15). The writer of the book of Acts also commends the Bereans for their studying in Acts 17:11, "Now these were more noble-minded than those in Thessalonica, for they received the word with great eagerness, examining the Scriptures daily to see whether these things were so."

As my mind reviews my memories of my beginnings with Lois, I can only hope that some sense of the love she had for the Lord, and the love she had for the Word of God is clear. I will always thank the Lord she said "yes" that first day I phoned her.

THREE
Revelations

Looking out my open window on a late spring afternoon, I see an expanse of green velvet grass and brightly coloured flowers. It is a perfectly beautiful day, sunny, warm, with a brilliant blue sky overhead. I am watching birds. My neighbour has a bird feeder in her yard, and there is a constant assortment of our feathered friends coming and going.

This scene reminds me of the large window over the kitchen sink that looked upon the backyard of the home where we lived when the children were growing up. While flipping through the pages of my mind, remembering the view from that window, I can still see the big chestnut tree and the row of lilac bushes across the back edge of the yard. I used to stand by that window and watch the birds. Many of my beginning experiences with the Lord came while living in that house. One of those early experiences was coming to terms with my anger problem.

I was unaware of the fact that I had a problem with anger, so I did not recognize the symptoms. When I came face to face with James 1:19-20: "This you know, my beloved brethren. But everyone must be quick to hear, slow to speak and slow to anger; for the anger of man does not achieve the righteousness of God." After reading these words, I realized that God had a lot of work to do in my heart.

Anger shows its face in many ways, but I did not always want to put the label "anger" on certain areas of my life. Anger can be demonstrated in frustration, or a grumpy and irritable attitude; it can display itself in self-pity, and my all-time-favorite was stony silence. If I got angry with Tom, I wouldn't speak for days, and, of course, our physical relationship would suffer.

The children were disciplined in anger. I ruled the house with the proverbial "iron fist." Oh, don't get me wrong; we had fun times. But when it came to obedience, my children were afraid of me. That truth still hurts me today. By the grace of God, I have told each one how sorry I am for the way I was and asked them to forgive me. As of today, all but one of them has. They love to tell my grandchildren that every kid in the neighborhood was afraid of me.

I was also a screamer, and when I got angry, I could be heard all over the neighbourhood. Believe me; I am not proud of any of this. When God began to convict me, and deal with me about my anger, I was devastated to learn how a loving mother and wife should be. I was absolutely broken over the magnitude of my failure.

When I looked at other people, I came off looking pretty good, but when I applied the standard that God has for a woman, and I began to see who I really was, realization hit me about just how wicked my heart could be. 2 Corinthians 10:12 says, "For we are not bold to class or compare ourselves with some of those who commend themselves; but when they measure themselves by themselves and compare themselves with themselves, they are without understanding." Jeremiah 17:9 calls our hearts desperately sick. "The heart is more deceitful than all else And desperately sick; who can understand it?" No one but God really understands how sick and deceitful the heart is.

There I was, and it was not a pretty picture. But God is gracious, and He remembers that we are dust (Psalm 103:14). Lois taught an awesome lesson on anger, filled with Scripture that I am still teaching today. "BE ANGRY, AND YET DO NOT SIN; do not let the sun go down on your anger, and do not give the devil an opportunity" (Ephesians 4:26, 27). "Let no unwholesome word proceed from your mouth, but only such a word as is good for edification according to the need of the moment, so that it will give grace to those who hear" (Ephesians 4:29). "Let all bitterness and wrath and anger and clamor and slander be put away from you, along with all malice" (Ephesians 4:31). I needed to recognize all forms of anger as sin.

Self-pity is another form of anger that I did not recognize as a problem. So much of my anger came from my feeling that I was being treated unfairly. My heart cried out that God was unfair. Life was too hard. I didn't deserve this. I deserved better than this. The Scripture is clear that God does not treat us as we should be treated because of our sin, but forgives our sin and deals with us out of love and compassion. There was no reason for me to feel sorry for myself.

> *He has not dealt with us according to our sins, Nor rewarded us according to our iniquities. For as high as the heavens are above the earth, So great is His lovingkindness toward those who fear Him. As far as the east is from the west, So far has He removed out transgressions from us. Just as a father has compassion on his children, So the Lord has compassion on those who fear Him (Psalm 103:10–13).*

In Psalm 32:1-2 David expresses how truly blessed he is when his sin has been forgiven by God and is not counted against him. Can you see why being angry about the circumstances of your life is such a slap in the face to God? He has given us His Son, and Jesus paid such a high price for our soul only to have us whine that He is unfair. The only answer for anger is to agree with God that it is sin, confess it, repent of it, and let God replace it with His love. There will be no victory over sin as long as we try to justify it.

Through the Lord's guidance I was invited to a Tim LaHaye seminar on *"The Four Spiritual Temperaments."* That was where I first discovered I was a sanguine. I struggle with strong emotions and tend to be reactionary. It was not surprising to learn that I had a problem with anger. This seminar helped me to understand why I react the way I do.

For many years I had let my feelings control me; now as a Christian, I was to let the Holy Spirit and the Word of God control me. Lois taught some incredibly simple spiritual truths. I found them simple, but not easy, and can still hear her say, "I must deliberately choose." Seeing the truth that "choosing" to obey the Word of God, and not choosing to do what I felt like doing, soon made a difference in my behavior based on this different way of thinking. Scripture defines this process as laying aside and putting on:

> that, in reference to your former manner of life, you lay aside the old self, which is being corrupted in accordance with the lusts of deceit, and that you be renewed in the spirit of your mind, and put on the new self, which in the likeness of God has been created in righteousness and holiness of the truth (Ephesians 4:22–24).

When I first heard this teaching it sounded hypocritical. It's like pretending to be something you are not. I thought that if I felt one way, but did another I would be seen as a phony.   But, we must remember that Jesus did not go to the cross because He felt like it.   The Scripture tells us that He ENDURED the cross, DESPISING the shame (Hebrews 12:2).   We also must remember His agony in the garden, where He prayed to have the cup taken away if it were possible (Matthew 26:39).   But Jesus walked in obedience to the Father's will, not letting His feelings control Him, and He walked in victory, pleasing the Father.   So it is with you and me.   As we choose to obey, regardless of how we feel, God does the changing in us, and soon we find our struggles with the habit of feelings lessen.   Oh, I blew it on many occasions.   But the miraculous was happening, and I found myself slowly losing my anger.   A change was taking place, and I loved it.

Over time I lost my sarcasm, I was less irritable and more patient; I didn't even scream as often, and that was really a miracle.   I was learning to love instead of rant and rave.   I'm sure my husband's thoughts were, "who is this woman, and where did my wife go?"   To say that this change in me had a profound effect on Tom is something I would love to be able to do, but, unfortunately, he had decided long before that if anything was my idea, he wanted nothing to do with it.   That attitude also applied to my Christianity.   But I never gave up hope that the changes God was making in me would someday make an impact on him.

No matter how much we learn there is always a new truth for a new day.   The next truth waiting for me was that I needed to obey God and His Word, and leave the results of my obedience with Him. God was examining my motives.   Why was I being obedient and wanting the changes in me?   Was it to have an easier life or was it really to please God?   I had to admit that I wanted Tom saved for me as well as for Him.

In my mind, I already had it all laid out how Tom was going to be saved, and he would become a sweet, loving, Christian husband, and my life would be so much better. When these motives came to light, I recognized that I needed to make some serious changes in my prayer life. I needed to pray for Tom's salvation for him, and for God's glory, and not for me. I began to pray a prayer that day that continued for twenty-five years. I daily asked God to work in whatever way was necessary to bring Tom to his knees in repentance and surrender. God answered that prayer, and later in my story I will share how. But for now, I don't want to get ahead of myself.

Lois's next major lesson was the love lesson. I needed to understand unconditional love, looking at how God loves me, and how He wants me to love others. This lesson I call "open heart surgery with no anesthetic." This one was painful. As I have said, I had compared myself with other women, and of course, they were the ones found wanting, not me.

This used to be a favorite line of mine: "I know I'm not the best housekeeper but you should see her house." (Sounds like a line from a soap opera.) God wants us to see others as He sees them, through His eyes. When God states in the familiar Scripture verse of John 3:16, that He so loved the world, He means all those others that we compare ourselves to. Lois took me to 1 Corinthians 13, the "love chapter." I am going to have to type through my tears as this memory comes flooding back.

My grief over my failure was complete. I cried for days. I had never loved Tom. I didn't even know what love was. My self-absorption had controlled every area of my life. I saw that I had not given one moment of my time to seeing things from Tom's perspective. I had never even tried to appreciate his good qualities, but only focused on his qualities that I perceived as bad. I had never showed him any love. He had not had any real love from his family, but now I could see that he had not had any love from his wife either.

The pain is almost unbearable when I remember what kind of a mother I was. I was definitely not nurturing, only demanding, and barking out orders like a drill sergeant. The children were given chores to do around the house. I would check their work, and if it didn't measure up to my standard, they would be made to go back and do it all over again. If they disobeyed, they were punished either by sending them to bed or taking away a privilege. Whatever action was taken, it was backed up by severe looks and harsh words in a raised voice.

The knowledge that I cannot undo any of my behaviour is still very painful to me. Thank God I don't let my mind go there very often. I know that the only answer for sin is to confess it and accept God's forgiveness; forgetting these sins is very hard. For the first time in my life, I saw what unconditional love was, true love. Not the love the world knows and thinks they want. It has nothing to do with emotion, but is action on our part. It is so totally unselfish; it can only be something that God does.

As the Word of God unfolded this Biblical role of wife to me, it broke me. God wants us to have a broken and a contrite heart (Psalm 51:17). Webster's dictionary defines the word broken as meaning "shattered" (1987, p. 181.). When Lois taught me the lesson on love, I was truly shattered. The definition of "contrite" is grieving and penitent for sin or short-coming (1987, p. 285). The word that fits me was "sin", because "shortcoming" was a little light for what I was seeing in myself. This was one time when I was so overwhelmed by my failure that I could have given up on myself, but once again God used His Word to encourage me.

Part of Israel's punishment for disobedience was pestilence. God had allowed hoards of locusts to strip them of their crops. Now we find through the prophet Joel, that God made them a wonderful promise,

> Then I will make up to you for the years That the swarming locust has eaten, The creeping locust, the stripping locust and the gnawing locust, My great army which I sent among you. You will have plenty to eat and be satisfied And Praise the name of the Lord your God, Who has dealt wondrously with you; Then my people will never be put to shame" (Joel 2:25–26).

The locusts had eaten away the years when my children were young. I no longer had an opportunity to raise them "in the discipline and instruction of the Lord" (Ephesians 6:4). But all was not lost. Just as God was loving, kind, and faithful to Israel, so He was with me. I was given an opportunity to stop my uncaring ways; praise His name. He has given me back the years the locusts had eaten.

I needed to confess to Tom what God had been teaching me. I didn't even know how to approach the situation because I knew that Tom couldn't possibly understand what God was doing in my heart. I prayed hard that God would give me the opportunity and the right words, and that He would prepare Tom's heart beforehand. I asked Tom to sit down with me one day and poured out my heart to him. I shared how God had convicted me about my selfishness. I asked him to forgive me for not appreciating what a good provider he was.

In spite of his drinking, Tom had always gone to work, even though he worked at a job that he hated. He worked the midnight shift on the railroad for many years and also worked part-time during the day painting houses. He never missed a mortgage payment and always paid our bills on time. We always had a nice home with plenty of food and decent clothes. He never complained about my cooking, my housekeeping, or how I disciplined the children. I never appreciated how hard it must have been for him that almost all of his paycheck went to care for our home and six children. I am sad to say that despite his dependability, there was no loving wife waiting for him at the door when he came home.

The dissatisfaction and loneliness that had dominated my life needed a source, and so the blame was laid squarely on Tom. I was not materialistic in the sense of wanting what I knew to be impossible, but I was never content with what I had. I wallowed in self-pity over his selfishness, never seeing my own. He loved baseball; I hated it. He liked to sleep late on his days off, and I wanted him up at the crack of dawn. I thought, "poor me" that I had to put up with him. We hardly ever even agreed about what TV show we would watch. I really believed all our problems were his fault. I wanted him to like what I liked and want what I wanted.

Our physical relationship also suffered; suffice to say it was not good. I had yet to learn that my body belonged to him, and so I had kept it to myself. I now recognized that I had wanted him to be someone he couldn't possibly be, and I didn't want who he really was. I needed to be changed. I needed to see him with God's unconditional love, to love him because God loved him, and Christ died for him.

Tom had always been a quiet man. He didn't talk much, and found it hard to talk about his personal feelings. Only when he had a few drinks did his tongue loosen. His reaction to my confession was quiet. I don't know what I expected from him. What I got was him talking about all my failings, and the fact that he saw me as I had seen him, as the one who was at fault. I don't think he ever did say he would forgive me, but God had set my feet on a new path, and I was staying there. By God's grace, I began to act as though I loved him, and slowly that love became real.

That day of our talk, started a new way of living for me. I made his favorite meals, made sure his bowling shirts were always clean and ready for him, smiled and said hello when he came home, gave him a kiss goodbye when he went to work (I tried to keep my complaining to a minimum), and made myself available to him physically, choosing to ignore how I felt. Do I sound like I became a saint? I apologize for that, because of course, that is not true. I struggled, but I persisted. When I read about the Apostle Paul's life, or the example of Jesus life, I know that mine had really been a piece of cake despite my feelings that life was so difficult for me.

We are admonished from the Word, "But I say, walk by the Spirit, and you will not carry out the desire of the flesh" (Galatians 5:16). I applied that truth. Just simply taking God at his Word, and believing He would do exactly what He said He would, that is faith. I chose to walk in obedience and, He supplied my needs. God gave me the love and strength to learn to live as a loving and submissive wife. It was me He was changing. Tom didn't change. But I liked the new me better. I discovered a new satisfaction was coming into my life. I was surprised to find that the more choices I made to please God, the more that discontentment and loneliness faded out of my life.

Jesus has promised us that "in Him" our joy will be full (John 15:11). We look to people and things to make us joyful and wonder why it doesn't happen. True joy exists only in Jesus. We place huge burdens on people with our expectations, when they can only be met in God. I had demanded something from Tom that he couldn't give me. But as I write this, I smile, knowing that because of this heart-breaking time, I learned a valuable lesson. God wants to make us into the image of His Son. That process means getting rid of my own right-eousness which my deceitful heart wants to keep. Remember, I called it "open heart surgery with no anesthetic." It can be excruciatingly painful, but is necessary for our good and God's glory.

FOUR
Proof

When the subject of trust comes up, the usual comment is that it must be earned. The Scriptures teach that God wants to gain our trust. He wants us to put Him to the test and prove that He is faithful. That is how we will learn that He is trustworthy. Proverbs is the book of wisdom, and it tells us, "He who gives attention to the word will find good, And blessed is he who trusts in the Lord" (16:20). Then the book of Psalms gives us the same instructions,

> *This poor man cried, and the Lord heard him And saved him out of all his troubles. The angel of the Lord encamps around those who fear Him, And rescues them. O taste and see that the Lord is good; How blessed is the man who takes refuge in Him! (Psalm 34:6-8)*

I was about to taste and see how good He was.

In the fall of 1974, Tom bought a new station wagon. It was a 1975 Ford. It was the first new car he had ever owned. He had it about five weeks, when I had to go to the doctor. I had found a lump in my breast, had an x-ray, and was going to find out the results. The lump was not malignant; the doctor told me it was only fatty tissue.

Coming home from my appointment that day, I drove down a street that had three lanes. I was driving in the middle lane, when all of a sudden, the car beside me on the driver's side, started to come over the line into my lane. I panicked and without looking yanked the wheel to my right and hit a car beside me. Thank the Lord, it was not a major accident, and I was not hurt, but my poor husband's new car had lost a bumper and had a nice "ding" in the rear. I was terrified to go home.

At that moment, I was really glad I was saved because I thought I might end up in heaven before the day was over when Tom found out about his car. He was home in bed sleeping after working a night shift blissfully unaware that his new car was not in the same shape it had been when he had come home from work. Needing to talk and looking for encouragement in this situation, I immediately called Lois. I was in tears.

It seemed to me that Tom was always angry. He had never used any excessive physical force with any of us, but the children and I were afraid of him and what he might do. He was very threatening at times, and the potential was there for him to do real harm to someone. I imagined looming disaster when I had to tell him about his car.

Lois, in her quiet gentle way, calmed me down and reminded me of some promises from the Bible I had been learning. Psalm 37:1-8, I learned, promises us that if we don't worry, trust in Him, rest in Him, and delight ourselves in Him, He will guard our way. She also reminded me of Isaiah 41:10 that the Lord would strengthen me and help me. I was glad to hear her say, "do not fear, for I am with you."

My spirit began to calm, and the fear began to ebb away. She talked to me for awhile, and prayed with me, urging me to keep my eyes on the Lord in this situation. She was so good to me, patiently listening when I would call her upset over something. I had a couple of hours before I had to wake Tom up, so I kept rereading the Scriptures and praying, "Please God, be in control of this situation."

We always lived on a fairly regular schedule, so every day we had our supper at about five o'clock. I would routinely wake Tom up about a half hour before we were ready to eat. I went up to our bedroom, woke him up, told him the time, and said, "I have good news, and I have bad news. Which one would you like to hear first?" He replied, "I'm not quite awake, so you better give me the good news first." I told him, "the lump in my breast is not malignant, and the doctor is fairly sure it's just fatty tissue." "Good, what's the bad news?" he asked. I took a deep breath, "I had an accident with the car." Just silence. "How bad was it?" So I described how it happened, and how much damage was done to the car. He didn't react, but just said, "Well, it's a good thing about your test, and that you're okay."

It's hard to describe how I felt that day. I was expecting this great angry explosion, and here was this quiet reaction. I was elated. I literally flew down the stairs. It seemed to me that my feet never even touched a step on the way down. I couldn't wait to get to the phone to call Lois. "You'll never believe what happened," I practically yelled into the phone. Always her calm self, she asked me to tell her.

Lois already knew what I needed to learn through my experience, that the Lord answers prayer, promising "I will never desert you, nor will I ever forsake you," (Hebrews 13:5). He is the God of the impossible. When the situation requires it, He does what is impossible for us to do. That experience of God's intervention began to teach me not to be afraid. God has intervened on my behalf many times since, but that is the memory that stands out in my mind at the beginning of this process of Him changing me. He has proven Himself over and over to me.

The bitterness, resentment, anger and fear were losing their hold on me, and I was learning a new way of life. God had given me a new perspective on my life, my marriage, and my children. It was like having a new pair of eyes. I learned a wonderful new truth. Thinking I didn't want my children, I had sought happiness elsewhere, and I also thought I would have been glad to be rid of Tom. But now, as time went on, I began to see how God treasures the family, to see that my children were priceless gifts from God, and that I was learning through my situation with Tom some exciting spiritual truths. I desperately wanted to somehow make up to Tom and my children for my past failures. But I discovered it wasn't so easy to do that. The children were such a blessing and able to accept the changes in me, but Tom could not forgive me.

Many times before my conversion, I had chosen a path that would turn out to be the wrong one. A few years before I came to the Lord, I had taken the children and skipped out in the middle of the night thinking that Tom would miss us so much that he would come to realize how much we meant to him. I thought that he would be so glad to have the children and me come back, that somehow our absence would change him. I had chosen the wrong path again. All he did was get angrier, and now I was living with the consequences of a very bad choice. I had to learn that God wanted me to be faithful in my role, and that my faithfulness was not dependant on how Tom chose to live, but that I was to live to please God.

The Bible gives very clear direction on how a wife should live, especially in Ephesians. "Wives, be subject to your own husbands, as to the Lord" (Ephesians 5:22). "and the wife must see to it that she respects her husband" (Ephesians 5:33). Peter writes in 1 Peter 3:1-6, that not only are wives to live in subjection to their husbands, but also that this command applies even if the husbands are not living in obedience to the Lord. Married couples today don't seem to see their marriage as a covenant relationship like the one described in Ephesians. They have forgotten, or did not understand in the first place, that they covenanted before God to be together until death.

We don't want God to break His covenant with us based on our victories or failures. We want to believe that no matter what our failures, He will forgive us and keep His word because of Christ's finished work on the cross. Our performance level doesn't determine God's faithfulness. But how do we treat our spouse? If his performance is not what we expect or want, do we immediately think of dissolving the relationship? The Apostle Paul instructs married couples that they should not leave their marriage, nor divorce their mates. "But to the married I give instructions, not I, but the Lord, that the wife should not leave her husband (but if she does leave, she must remain unmarried, or else be reconciled to her husband), and that the husband should not divorce his wife (1 Corinthians 7:10–11).

My marriage relationship was unequally yoked. We were both unsaved when we came into it, but now things had changed. There are limited Scripture passages about being unequally yoked, but the instruction is clear. 1 Corinthians 7:12-15, simply says the believer shall not leave the marriage. The result of this obedience the Bible says is that the spouse is sanctified by the believer, and your children are made holy. Webster's dictionary defines sanctified to mean "set apart to a sacred purpose" (1987, p. 1040). God has a holy purpose for the believer to stay in the marriage and not dissolve it just because it is difficult. If, however, the unbelieving spouse chooses to leave, then the believer is instructed to let him or her go, and the believer is no longer bound to that covenant. It was clear to me where God wanted me.

The thing that amazed me so much in this whole process of learning God's will for me was that I was experiencing peace, joy, love and satisfaction. Tom had not changed. My circumstances had not changed. But I was seeing an incredible difference in me. Now this may not seem as amazing to you as you read this as it was for me, but the despair was gone, and in tasting the goodness of God, I found it delicious.

The terrible emptiness I had lived with for so long was disappearing. I recognized I had always looked to other people for my significance and value. Now I was beginning to really experience God's love and care. Tom was still angry with me all the time and hardly ever at home. I was dealing with four teenagers and two younger children, mostly on my own. Tom supplied our financial needs, but almost all the rest was on my shoulders. But I was seeing it all very differently from the early years of our marriage. Oh, my days still ranged between victory and defeat. The discouragement was still a battle. It was the old one step forward and two steps back spiritual dance, but praise God, the despair was gone. Let me take you on to the next story of God's wonderful protection, provision and proof.

July 7, 1975 was a lovely summer day. The kids had been out of school for a week on summer vacation. I had taken the car in for a tune up, with my oldest son, and Nancy, my oldest daughter, was home with the rest of our children. Tom, as usual, was in bed sleeping after working a night shift. As I recall, it was about 11 a.m. when I arrived home. Nancy came running down the front porch steps crying that our youngest daughter Barbara, the baby of the family, had been hit by a car. She was seven at the time. A neighbour boy had come to the house to tell us that Barbara was trying to cross the street with our bicycle when she was hit.

The kids had only one bike to share. One of our sons had taken it to his friend's home about a block away, on a very busy street. Barbara was allowed to ride it only in the schoolyard across the street and not on the street itself. It was her turn to have the bike, so she had gone to get it. She was wheeling it back to the schoolyard and had walked right out in front of a car. This accident was not the driver's fault.

Nancy woke up her dad, and he ran in bare feet, with only his pants on to where Barbara was lying in the road. A neighbour had called the ambulance and covered her with a blanket. The neighbours told me later that Tom had gotten down on the pavement and curled up beside her until help arrived. See: he had his good qualities. He rode to the hospital in the ambulance with Barb.

Dropping off my son, I immediately turned the car around and headed for the hospital. I drove and prayed. Two of my five verses popped into my head. They were 1 Corinthians 10:13, and Romans 8:28. "God, you have promised me that you won't give me more than I can bear. I trust you for the grace and strength to face whatever will be at the hospital when I get there. I just believe your Word that 'All things work for good to those who love you.'" Thank God for Lois and her faithful teaching of the Word of God. I really had no idea what was ahead of me.

The hospital was not far. I raced into the emergency room; the first thing I saw was this young man sitting there sobbing. When I asked the nurse where Barbara was, he asked, "Are you her mother?" I said "yes." He sobbed out the words "I'm so sorry; she ran right in front of my car." I felt so sorry for him; I told him I would come back to let him know how she was as soon as I knew anything, and that I understood that the accident was not his fault. When I recall this, I can hardly believe that in this situation, I would be consoling the driver and later even went back to him to let him know how Barbara was. It was all of God's doing.

Barbara was lying on a table crying. Her dad was right there beside her, holding her hand. There was a team of doctors and nurses all around her. They were putting her up in traction, and the sight of her broke my heart. Barb was a small girl; she was all battered and bruised, her little face was all scraped, and there was still blood coming from her nose and ears.

When God tells us, "My grace is sufficient for you, for power is perfected in weakness" (2 Corinthians 12:9), He means just that, for it was only His grace that kept me from falling apart and bursting into tears. Barb's left leg was black from hip to knee, and swollen twice its normal size. Her femur bone (the thick bone in the top part of the leg) had broken completely in two about an inch from her hip joint, and it had hemorrhaged badly. She had lost a lot of blood, and the medical staff could not yet tell if she had any internal injuries.

As I struggle to recapture these memories, I feel sad to remember that Tom and I could not lean on each other because of the distance in our relationship. He hung on to Barbara, and I hung on to the Lord, amazed at how calm He kept me.

The medical team hung Barb up in traction by both legs, with her little bottom about an inch off the bed. There were ropes and pulleys going every which way. She cried and cried, but they finally gave her something for the pain, and she drifted off to sleep. It was the beginning of a very long six months of pain and trauma for her. I learned to trust and pray.

In studying the Bible over the years from the beginning of Genesis to the end of Revelation, I have found many great and precious promises, but I have never come across a verse that gives an easy answer to why God works in our lives the way He does. The only real explanation for what He is doing comes from the Book of Isaiah, where God reveals some of Himself to Israel.

In Isaiah 55, God, through the prophet, tells Israel to come to Him, to listen to Him, to seek Him while He can be found, and to call upon Him while He is near. They are encouraged to forsake their wicked ways and return to Him. If they do this, Israel is promised that God will have compassion on them and will pardon their sin. Then God reveals a little about Himself and tells us in verses 8-13 that we cannot understand His ways. He has a good purpose in everything He does, but His ways are beyond our understanding. "For My thoughts are not your thoughts, Nor are your ways My ways," declares the Lord. "For as the heavens are higher than the earth, So are My ways higher than your ways And My thoughts than your thoughts" (Isaiah 55:8–9).

These are the boundaries we must work and live within. God has set them in place. How high are the heavens above the earth? When we are faced with this question, we have no choice but to be still. We cannot answer it. We can only trust and believe, and that is exactly what God wants us to do. Four different times in Scripture, once in the Old Testament, and three times in the New Testament, we are told the righteous man shall live by his faith (Habakkuk 2:4, Romans 1:17, Galatians 3:11, Hebrews 10:38). That's the only answer we have to our "why Lord?"

From Lois's teaching, I learned 1 Thessalonians 5:18, "in everything give thanks; for this is God's will for you in Christ Jesus." This command to us does not say "feel thankful", but "give" thanks. It calls for obedience not emotions. Again we find a Biblical command that is simple but not easy.

Barb was in traction for eleven days, and during that time a young boy who also was a patient came into her room and asked what all the pulleys and ropes were for. While I was standing there, he reached up and turned one of the knobs holding the ropes in place and her broken leg fell down. She let out a scream, and we immediately called for a nurse who put her leg back up where it belonged. It's difficult giving thanks in all things, and it was hard watching her go through this. When the doctors x-rayed her again to see how the break was healing, they found it had not joined at all. The medical team decided to try casts. Barbara was put in a cast from her waist to her ankles, on both legs, open in the centre so she could use the bathroom. Now it was another wait and see for ten to fourteen days.

Quickly exhaustion set in from going back and forth to the hospital and seeing Barbara hurting and homesick, but my eldest daughter carried a much larger load. It was summer holidays, and her four brothers were out of school. She took on the greater part of my role that summer. She was nineteen, and the boys were seventeen, fifteen, eleven, and nine. Barbara never wanted me to leave the hospital. There have been many times I have been truly thankful for Nancy, and this was definitely one of those times. God's constant blessings are all around us; we need only to look for them. They are right in front of us, in our spouse, our children, and in our extended family.

The next x-ray also showed that the bones were not knitting at all. Now what? The only alternative left to the doctors was surgery. They explained to Tom and me that they would have to put a metal plate in Barb's leg held there by screws, to join the two pieces of bone.

Lois and I had daily communication, and she always pointed me back to the Word of God and His promises. I held on to that and prayed desperately from a mother's heart, bathed in a mother's tears. I know that God hears a mother's prayer for her child. He had heard my mother's prayers for me, and now He was listening to mine for Barbara. You do not know what you can bear until He walks through the valley with you.

Barbara had to be cut out of the cast before the doctors could operate. I had never seen this done before. They used a little power saw, and ran it up each side of both legs. Barbara was frightened and crying, and I just stood by her head holding on to her hands, and cried with her, and prayed. I know they did not hurt her, although I did think the vibrations from the saw might have made her broken leg hurt a bit. The next day they did the surgery on her, and she came through it fine, but she had the casts back on.

We spent the better part of two months at the hospital. Two of our children have birthdays in July, and so we had a big birthday party there. We brought the cake and ice cream, balloons and other decorations to the hospital, and had some of the children and the some of the staff come to celebrate with us. Once the surgery was over, Barbara was much better. She was bedridden, but we made fun times with her. The driver of the car came regularly to see her and to bring her gifts. Barbara came home in September.

Over the next four months, Barbara had a tutor at home to keep her up with school. Her leg eventually healed, the casts came off, and then she managed crutches until she could finally walk again. She returned to school after the Christmas break. Her ordeal had lasted six months. Today she has a nasty scar and still has the plate and screws at her hip. But I recognize God's amazing grace that taught me that if we let Him, He will prove Himself faithful to His Word. It could have been much worse.

We do not always see the results of things God allows in our lives, but one special thing that happened to me at the hospital sticks in my memory. The head nurse on the children's ward came into Barbara's room to visit one day, and said she was amazed at how well she had done. Barbara had stayed pretty sweet-tempered throughout her ordeal.

Then she said, "I know that is because of how calm and steady you have been. We have been watching you, and you have been a rock. Most parents come in here, and when their children are going through a rough time, the parents can cause the kids problems because they are so upset in front of them. You never did that once." I am thankful to the Lord that He had already changed me from the angry, outspoken mom I had been. I could hardly imagine what the nurse's perception would have been of the old me. I give all the credit to the Lord. He kept His Word, gave me His strength and His help, and never gave me more than I could bear just as He promised.

You never know when you are a testimony for the Lord, or when people are watching to see your reaction. I told the nurse that the Lord had been my strength, that I had been in constant prayer, and also that many others were praying for us. God "proved" His grace truly is sufficient.

FIVE
Just Walking

Most of the time we had an average life, and there was no high drama. We were like many other families living from day to day, coping with completing homework assignments, sibling rivalry, and sporting events. We also shared some great fun times. For me, a good number of the fun times were at the beach.

"Beach Bum" is a label that has been attached to me for most of my life. My idea of the perfect summer was to lay in the sun, by the lake, work on a tan, swim, read a book, and do basically nothing. Everybody has dreams, and mine was to own a cottage where I would spend these perfect summers. Alas, it was not to be. Instead, I drove my poor husband crazy because there was always a ton of sand in the car from carting the kids to the beach.

Tom was fair-skinned and easily became sunburned, so my idea of the perfect summer was not the same as his. His idea was to sit in the house all summer with cold beer and baseball on TV. YUK! We were so incompatible. It's funny how you don't see these things when you're sixteen and "so in love."

The summer before Barbara's accident, Tom bought the family a swimming pool. It was an above ground style, four feet deep and twenty-four feet in diameter. (I guess after about the tenth ton of sand he cleaned out of the car, he had enough.) My idea of a perfect summer needed to be changed. This time it was poolside, working on a tan, swimming, and reading a good book. Hey, that wasn't such a bad idea.

He built a deck around the outside, and made a jumping in spot for the kids out of the stump of a large old chestnut tree we had to cut down to put up the pool. The kids, the dog, named Sarge, and I, had many fun times together in that pool. I have nagged them to destroy unforgiving pictures of me in a tube in the pool, but to no avail. I have wonderful memories of those days. We had some great summers in the backyard. During those summers I was still meeting weekly with Lois.

Lois and I were concentrating on abundant living. I wanted to understand and experience "walking in the Spirit" in my moment by moment, day to day living without falling.

God's Word tells us we say things like,

> Come now, you who say, "Today or tomorrow we will go to such and such a city, and spend a year there and engage in business and make a profit." Yet you do not know what your life will be like tomorrow. You are just a vapor that appears for a little while and then vanishes away. Instead, you ought to say, "If the Lord wills, we will live and also do this or that." (James 4:13–15)

Spiritually speaking, I've had some nasty falls. Looking back on my day to day living, it seems to me that there was constant daily work of dealing with my attitude.

"Attitude" ranks right up there with "submission" as the two least favourite words we can hear, especially as Christian women. Sometimes you just want to scream, "Leave me alone!" I have screamed that on occasion, but certainly not where anyone can hear me. I felt picked on. Self-pity was a struggle. I wanted God to deal with Tom, so my life would be easier. But having it easier was not God's goal in my life, changing me was His goal. What I needed to do was surrender myself fully to God and let Him renew my mind (Romans 12:1– 2). You've probably heard it said that Christianity is a woman's religion. It's just a crutch for us to lean on because we are weak. From this page I would like to shout "absolutely not." It is the hardest work in the world to die to self and live to please God.

Tom and I were legally married, but a oneness in our marriage did not exist. The only thing that we shared was the same street address. We had perfunctory communication, and our physical relationship, (I should just say contact, because there was no relationship) was rare, and only if Tom had been drinking. I tried to keep my focus on my role, as a submissive wife and loving mother, with constant prayers for God to give me the love I needed for Tom.

Seeing Tom through God's eyes was what I needed, and it was impossible for me in my own strength. Only God could do this thing in me. Praise Him that He is the God of the impossible. Jesus said in John 15:5 "for apart from Me you can do nothing." I had to see Tom as one that God created, and one that Jesus died for. I needed the same compassion for Tom that Jesus had for the lost. If you do a study of the word "compassion" in all the Gospels, you will find that Jesus, over and over, had compassion on people and that compassion motivated Him to heal, teach, and even raise the dead. He saw them as sheep without a shepherd, wandering and lost (Matthew 9:36). Too many times all I saw was a man I couldn't stand the sight of.

Lois continued to faithfully teach the truth of God's Word. Seeing almost no results at home in my relationship with Tom, my battle with discouragement raged. God drew my attention to Paul's letter to the Galatians in which he writes "Let us not lose heart in doing good, for in due time we will reap if we do not grow weary" (Galatians 6:9).

The Scriptures also spoke to me when Jesus said in Luke 6:46 "Why do you call Me, 'Lord, Lord' and do not do what I say?" I kept walking through my days, one foot in front of the other, sometimes to failure, sometimes to victory, but the greatest thing was, I kept on walking. One of my great joys was to see change in me: one of my old habit patterns was not finishing things. The "old me" was a quitter. Praise God, not anymore.

Tom was rarely home except to sleep. When he did show up he had usually been drinking heavily. My life involved church activities and being with the children. Leaving him for good ate away at me, but that still small voice kept repeating, "The believer shall not leave" (1 Corinthians 7: 13).

I am so thankful for God's grace and strength that held me up so that I never packed it in. A familiar phrase that comes to my mind is "nothing in life that is worthwhile is ever easy." I'm not sure where I heard it or read it, but it sits there in my memory. The operative word in that statement is "worthwhile." I believe that every time we walk in light of the Word of God there is eternal value in obeying it. Jesus said "If you love Me, you will keep My commandments" (John 14:15). Loving God means obedience to the Word. Matthew tells us, "YOU SHALL LOVE THE LORD YOUR GOD WITH ALL YOUR HEART" (Matthew 22:37). Maybe today as you read this you are going through rough waters. I can assure you that our Heavenly Father knows where you are, no matter how deep or dark the valley. Psalm 139 gives us the assurance of how intimately acquainted He is with us, and all our steps as we walk through our days. He always has a good purpose in all His dealings with us.

Over the next couple of years our relationship deteriorated further. Our home became a tense place of fear whenever Tom was around. His anger seemed to have no limit, and we went through some very frightening moments. It accomplishes nothing to go into the details of those times, so I just want to give the Lord all the praise, the honor, and the glory for His protection and care because no one ever got hurt. Tom never hurt me or the children.

Lois had become my lifeline. I know that Jesus is to be our all in all, but I am firmly convinced that He fleshes out His love and sufficiency to us through people. He places that special someone in our life that will hug us, hold our hand, and listen when we need to pour out our hearts. Jehovah-jireh means "the Lord will provide." The title comes from Genesis 22:14 which records Abraham naming the place where God provided the ram for the sacrifice, so Abraham did not have to sacrifice his son Isaac. God had provided Lois for me. I'm sure that you have been there in that place also, where you have thought you would not have gotten through without that special person the Lord provided.

In many ways it was humanly impossible to live in our home during those dark days. God's special gift to me for that time was Lois' ability to "speak the truth in love." I cried to her most of the time, but she always steered me back to the Word. She pointed me away from looking at my home situation, and back to getting my eyes on the Lord. Whatever the question, her answer was always the Lord. It was, I can do all things through Him (Philippians 4:13), give thanks in all things (1

Thessalonians 5:18), God is faithful (1 Thessalonians 5:24), and abide in Christ (John 15). I wanted sympathy, but she gave me truth. She was a gift to me, straight from the hand of God.

1980 dawned and I was extremely concerned about Tom's drinking. But there was something else nagging at me. A little niggling down deep inside that I couldn't put my finger on. Tom was gone so much; he was not even home nights on the weekends now. I had confronted him once about him seeing another woman, but he had just brushed it off saying, "don't worry about it." I would have run away if I could have seen what was coming at me down the road. It was one of those things that we think happens by chance. Only when God is in it, I don't think anything happens by "chance."

Tom had a bowling buddy named John. Bowling was Tom's life now, and he bowled seven days a week. He was supposed to be leaving very early one morning for a bowling trip, so he told me that he had decided to stay overnight at John's. He had parked a little yellow car in our driveway and took our station wagon. I was to get the car back before he left. The exact reason escapes me, but something came up and I needed to talk to him. I phoned John's.

John was vague on the phone when I asked to speak to Tom. He made a half-hearted attempt at excuses, but when I nailed him down about another woman, he caved. Tom had not been at John's at all. This was the first time I heard about his girlfriend. I did not know that Tom had been having an affair for three and a half years. I found out later that the little yellow car belonged to her. Unless you have been there, you cannot understand the terrible humiliation infidelity causes. I wanted to die. There was a dark tunnel looming in front of me, and the only choice I was being given was to walk through it.

SIX

Endings Come...

One of the wonderful blessings of living on the shore of Lake Huron is the sunsets. Standing with my back to the east and facing west, I look out over the vast expanse of blue water and it's like looking at a postcard designed for tourists. I'm often puzzled by the fact that people who live here still travel many miles to see beaches and oceans when they have such beauty here at home.

This place where I live is called "Bluewater Land." In the daytime there is a colour range in the lake, which, depending on the depth of the water, goes form a blue-green turquoise to a deep royal blue. A canvas could hardly display the colour this lake gives us with natural beauty.

The lake is usually filled with boats of all descriptions, but the ones that stand out the most in sharp contrast to the water's colour are the sailboats. They skim along the top of the water with their colourful spinnakers flying against the wind. It's a sight to behold. By evening, people begin to flock to the shore, knowing that they will be witnesses to the gorgeous sunset that will come.

The sun begins to fall in a fiery ball to the edge of the horizon, and as it appears to slowly drop off the edge of the world, the colours splay them-selves across the sky. Streaks from the palest pink, to the brightest fuchsia light up the early evening. The ball continues to descend, and the colours change to shades of gold, orange, and red. It's like looking at the autumn trees; you never get tired of that picture. I tell people that it is even more beautiful when you know the painter personally. Then in an instant, the colour is gone. Darkness drops down as if someone has pulled a shade. Day has ended once again. Endings come. It is a part of living that things must come to an end, and sometimes that includes marriage.

Tom and I never really had a marriage, as many couples do, but when the end came, it was still very difficult and painful. From my experience, I have come to understand that there is a spiritual process in the marriage relationship designed by God. When He says, "For this reason a man shall leave his father and his mother, and be joined to his wife; and they shall become one flesh" (Genesis 2:24), that something that God does in this special union is more than just physical. God creates a oneness that we humanly cannot explain. The pain of ending it is like trying to rip your arm out of its socket. It is excruciating.

It is easier to look back on the end of our marriage from today's vantage point. The pain is gone, and I have developed through my faith the ability to see Tom without bitterness and anger. Because of the emptiness of our marriage, I was astounded by the pain that the knowledge of his affair caused me.

The phone call that revealed the truth, gave me not only pain, but also some relief. My first reaction was "now I can dump him." I immediately set in place plans to "get out." I phoned Lois. She of course directed my attention to the Bible. To my dismay at the time, I was soon to learn that my plans did not fit into God's plan.

Jesus seems to give us a reason to divorce when He gives us the exception clause in Matthew 19:9, "And I say to you, whoever divorces his wife, except for immorality," so I thought I would be easily justified leaving Tom. But just because He gives us that option does not mean we must take it. He may know that staying in the situation is choosing the better path. His still small voice kept whispering in my ear: "the believer will not leave."

Now the perfect way for you and I to handle these situations is how Mary handled it when the angel told her she was to become pregnant with Jesus when she was not married yet. Her response was Luke 1:38: "And Mary said, "Behold, the bondslave of the Lord; may it be done to me according to your word. And the angel departed from her." I have to be honest and tell you that I did not handle my situation as well as Mary did at the start.

The argument with God lasted about two weeks. He would whisper in His still small voice, and I would give Him all my reasons why I did not have to do what He wanted me to do. God wanted me to stay with Tom, in spite of the situation, and I was determined that I was going to leave him. It seemed like all my headway in loving Tom was lost, and I hated him again.

Those days were like riding a spinning top. Stop the world! I want to get off! I ranged in emotions from hysterical crying, to angry outbursts, and to outright rebellion. Lois, as always, in her consistent, gentle, and persuasive manner continued to point me to the Lord and His Word. As in my past experiences, after much struggle, through the Word of God, I arrived at spiritual victory. I want to give you a snapshot of one of my dark days that caused that struggling.

Two of our children, who were both married by this time, had their own homes. Unbeknownst to me, they were aware of Tom's comings and goings because they had been following their father. They came in the door one day, both very upset. They had followed Tom to his girl-friend's apartment building and saw her with their dad. Tom and his girlfriend were coming out the door with their arms around each other. Not having any comprehension of how this would affect me, they poured out all their anger in a torrent.

The mind does weird and wonderful things to us at times, and mine gave me a very detailed picture of my husband with this other woman. I completely fell apart. I was so devastated; I could not stop the deep gut-wrenching sobs that came. I ran upstairs to my room. Over and over I kept repeating to myself, "not my Tom, not my Tom."

Only someone who has experienced infidelity can understand the depth of the suffering you go through. Something that I had not perceived as valuable was gone, and my sense of loss was overwhelming. I could not understand why the pain was so great. What I understood later was that the one flesh union was being ripped to shreds, and it was a painful process.

The Old Testament gives us the record of Israel's adultery against God. Again and again, we read that Israel committed fornication and played the harlot. They walked in unfaithfulness, intermarried with pagans, and worshipped false gods (2 Chronicles 21:11, Isaiah 23:17–18). The prophets were sent to her with the message, stop your unfaith-fulness and return to your God, (Jeremiah 3:11–14). Then Jeremiah records the pain that Israel's unfaithfulness caused God, as God laments over their adultery. "My soul, my soul! I am in anguish! Oh, my heart! My heart is pounding in me;" (Jeremiah 4:19).

Through my heartbreak, Lois just pointed me back to the Scrip-tures. It was her gentleness and the still small voice of God that brought me to the place of surrender. I was physically and emotionally exhausted when I fell on my knees and finally said yes to the Lord. "O.K. Lord," I wept. "I will stay here to please you and be obedient, but I can't do this in my own strength. You have to do this in me." For three months, I lived with Tom who was sleeping at home during the week, and every weekend leaving on Friday after work, and not coming home until Sunday night. He spent all his weekends at his girlfriend's place.

The next three months in this broken marriage were not easy; it was a very emotional time. But to my joy and amazement, I discovered that I had learned to make Jesus and His Word my foundation. I was stronger in Him than I had ever imagined I could be. I anticipated agony but received victory. God had kept His promise that He would do it in me. Philippians 4:13 was true. When God's will for us is difficult, He will supply everything we need to be obedient. In 2 Corinthians 4:7 we read, "But we have this treasure in earthen vessels, so that the surpassing greatness of the power will be of God and not from ourselves;". He alone has the right to all the glory.

Victory doesn't mean free of pain. You can walk in the Spirit while the tears flow. Remember, Jesus wept outside Lazarus' tomb (John 11:35), yet the Scripture teaches He was without sin (Hebrews 4:15). I cried a lot and prayed, and Lois cried with me, and prayed for me. God had set my feet on a path, and that didn't change. Tom never budged in his stubbornness. But I was learning that obedience is the path to victory.

Lois had been teaching me the Word of God for nearly five years when my marriage completely disintegrated. I had learned some wonderful principles:

1. I deliberately choose to obey in spite of my feelings or circumstances.

2.   I must leave the results of my obedience to God.

3.   I must give thanks in "all" things.

4.   The Holy Spirit will guide me according to the Word, never against it.

5.   I must praise the Lord at all times, even during the dark ones.

In Isaiah 61:3 God's Word tells us that for those who mourn there is comfort, "Giving them a garland instead of ashes, The oil of gladness instead of mourning, The mantle of praise instead of a spirit of fainting." I was truly thankful, not for my situation, but for my foundation. Remember the Scripture says, "Oh taste and see that the Lord is good" (Psalm 34:8). I was at the banquet table.

The beginning of July 1980 rolled around, and a friend of mine offered me her cottage for a few weeks to get away from my home situation. It seemed like most of the time the tension in the house was so bad I could literally "cut the air with a knife." To this day, I am not sure whether my decision to go was a good one or not, but the kids and I went to the lake. As soon as we were gone, Tom moved in with his girlfriend. I took only enough clothes for us to be away a short time, and my intention never was to leave him.

At the end of the month we came home after hearing about Tom's move. The grief over our loss was overwhelming. Tom was gone, and for the first time in my life, I was alone. I had gone from my parent's home to life with Tom. I had little education, having quit school in grade ten. I had never supported myself, let alone a family, and there were still four of our kids at home. How could all this possibly work out for good? One of the things I still had to learn about the Lord was that He had a plan!

The end of one thing is the new beginning of another. Joanna Weaver in her book, *Having a Mary Heart in a Martha World* writes, "Sometimes the story of our lives seems like one painful episode after another" (2000, p. 134). Further on the same page she writes, "Though Jesus knows our triumphant outcomes, though He sees the joyful ending just around the bend, He still gets down in the middle of our sorrow and holds us close, mingling His tears with our own" (2000, p. 134). I realized that a chapter of my life was ending, but as I had already learned, endings do bring new beginnings.

SEVEN

...Beginnings Follow

Beginnings make me think of the creation account in the book of Genesis. Close your eyes and come with me back to the very beginning. Are your eyes closed? Everything is dark. The Scripture says, "The earth was formless and void, and darkness was over the surface of the deep" (Genesis 1:2). Then God began creating. He separated the day from the night. He set the sun in the daytime sky. Generations have come and gone and still the sun hangs there, never moving an inch since that day. It is still hanging where God placed it that fourth day of creation. He set the moon and the stars in their places also to light the night.

Look really hard at the full moon, and the shadows give the image of a smiling face. You know him: it's the "man in the moon." Look up again into the night sky. Do you see the stars? God is the jeweler who opened His bag of diamonds and scattered them on black velvet across the universe. See how they twinkle and sparkle as they reflect the sun's rays. The psalmist writes, "He counts the number of the stars; He gives names to all of them" (147:4). How wonderful it must have been to have watched our world come into being.

Each day holds expectations and excitement, in itself a brand new creation. God has given us a day that has never been here before, and will never be here again. "This is the day which the Lord has made; Let us rejoice and be glad in it (Psalm 118:24).

Today when I got up, it was very gray and overcast with a light rain falling. The birds were still singing, but there was no lovely sunshine to start the day. Beginnings can be like that. If I had control over the weather, I would have every day about 25° C (77° F), sunny, with a slight breeze lazily moving the leaves. All nature that needs water to grow would die of thirst because I don't want dark rainy days. That's the way I am with life. Could I please have just a nice, easy, continuous stretch of days with no complications, difficulties or pain? Thank you very much!

But God loves us. He understands that just as nature needs the rain, so do we. We need the storms of life to strengthen our foundations or deepen our roots. It is in the crises that people act. Look at your own experience. When do you fall on your knees and cry out to God? Usually, it is when you are faced with the impossible. You could be faced with times of terminal illness, death, serious accident, financial ruin, natural disaster, divorce, and the list goes on and on. None of us knows what tomorrow holds. We can read how David cries out to God time and time again in the Psalms, as his enemies seek to slay him, and then writes, "Before I was afflicted I went astray, But now I keep Your word" (Psalm 119:67). Just as David had learned that it was good for him to go through difficulty, I too was faced with learning this same lesson.

All of a sudden my world was turned upside down. So much of what had been familiar to me was gone. The children and I were still living in the house, but I had changed the bedrooms around. I couldn't bear to have the same bedroom that Tom and I had shared. I didn't go out very much; I was afraid of bumping into Tom with another woman.

By September, when the kids went back to school, God provided a job for me at the local Christian book store. It was only part-time, but that was all I could handle at the time. The first few months of adjustment to my new lifestyle were made up of getting through one day at a time. Lois was a bottomless source of encouragement always pointing to the Lord as my strength. She knew what I needed as I faced this movement out of my comfort zone and into strange new territory.

Christmas eventually came, but it was not "Happy Holidays" at our house. The thing that sticks in my mind about it was Christmas dinner. I had cooked our traditional turkey dinner as I had every year. But that year everyone ate very little. Tom had come by on Christmas Eve and brought gifts for the kids, but had only stayed for a short time. It was upsetting for them. The days were dark, and I was waiting on the Lord to put the sun back in my sky.

Barbara's first bout of sickness came in January 1981. I thought she had the flu. Another beginning was upon me, but that realization was to come much later.

In the spring, I received a phone call. It was from a woman I had worked with on a political campaign to try to help get a Christian man elected to Parliament. She called to tell me she was leaving her job at the small claims court and wanted to recommend me for the job. She knew of my circumstances, and that I needed full-time employment.

Applying for the small claims court position meant facing more "beginnings." I would have to switch hats from full-time homemaker, to full-time employment, and mom and homemaker when I could muster up the energy. I looked around hoping to find a time machine so I could go back to the life that I was comfortable with. Doesn't that sound a lot like Israel wanting to go back to Egypt? Nevertheless God supplied and I was hired for the clerk typist position.

Picturing me as a "career" woman was never how I saw myself. There were no student loans to help lower income students achieve post-secondary education when I was young, so I expected to get married and have a family. Being the breadwinner as well as mom and homemaker was not what I would have chosen for myself if given the option. The hardest thing to accept in all of this was the fact that my time with Lois had come to an end. Because of her age, she did not teach in the evenings, so our time together had to stop now that I was working full-time.

The job at the small claims court office required me to spend my days typing. Typing has never been my strong suit. I failed it in grade nine, and didn't take it in grade ten. I had taken a typing course again at the high school years later and only succeeded in humiliating myself again by failing. To say that I disliked typing is putting it in a nice way, because truly my feelings are a lot stronger about it than that.

I was learning to trust the Lord for "everything" and "pray about everything" (Philipians 4:6–7). I would sit on the toilet seat at work and cry and pray, asking the Lord to be in control, and telling Him I knew He knew how to type. I can laugh about it now, but I wasn't laughing then; I was very serious. I really needed His help.

Barbara kept getting sick with the "flu." My going to work full-time was hard on her. She was only twelve. Back and forth we went to the doctor, but each time they found nothing. Nearly a year went by, and Barb was losing weight, and constantly sick with very bad headaches, vomiting, and diarrhea. The doctor decided she had migraine headaches as a result of the stress of her father leaving our home.

One day she was so sick, I called the doctor in tears, but he just yelled at me over the phone that he was absolutely sure her problems were psychological. I asked for psychology tests to be done to see if that was true. The test results showed that Barbara had no psychological problems. Through this process I met Monica, her psychologist. God had replaced Lois in my life.

EIGHT
Intervention

The Scripture says "The steps of a man are established by the Lord, And He delights in his way. When he falls, he shall not be hurled headlong, Because the Lord is the One who holds his hand" (Psalm 37:23–24). The walk day-by-day that God gives us is personally designed for us. I believe this to be the absolute truth simply because I would not have chosen the path I was walking if the choice had been mine.

Monica spent quite some time with me going over Barb's tests to show me how she had arrived at the conclusion that Barb's problems were physical. Barb and I saw her on and off for a few weeks, and as I became more comfortable with her, I realized how much I needed her listening ear. She, like Lois, was of a quiet spirit and gentle nature.

Barbara was getting worse, and people were beginning to notice that she looked really ill. She was underweight and had "flu" symptoms continually. Still her doctor would not take her illness seriously, even with the results of the psychology tests. Praise God, He would intervene for me once again. Into my life came Dr. Lillian Beatty.

Dr. Beatty had been a medical missionary in the Congo for many years. A severe case of malaria had brought her back to Canada. After her treatment, she was well enough to return to work, and had taken a job at one of our local hospitals. Our church became her church home, and much to my surprise, she befriended me.

Now you may ask "why would that surprise you?" Picture this: Dr. Beatty had never been married, was the only child of Christian parents, was financially well off, was an educated professional, and was a number of years my senior. You have read about my background and experience, and no two people could have been more unlikely to be friends. When the circumstances are extraordinary, that's the place God works.

God reveals Himself in His miraculous works. In the situations that are out of our hands as humans, God steps in and does the impossible for us. Jesus tells the unbelieving Jews in John 10:38, "though you do not believe Me, believe the works, so that you may know and understand that the Father is in Me, and I in the Father." When God takes control of a situation that we have no control over, the results reveal that He has done the miraculous.

One Sunday after church, Dr. Beatty invited me out to lunch. At the restaurant, I broke down and told her I was convinced that Barbara was dying, but her doctor wouldn't listen to me. At her insistence, I filled her in on what was going on with Barbara and described her symptoms. I told her that something was very wrong with Barbara's pigment, and that she was getting extremely dark looking, with the pressure points on her body being even darker. Dr. Beatty asked if she could see her, and so she came to my home and met her. As she was leaving, she asked my permission to talk with Barbara's doctor. Crying, I told her to go ahead, that I was desperate for someone to do something. After talking to Dr. Beatty, Barbara's doctor admitted her to the hospital for testing.

In the Congo, Dr. Beatty had seen a number of cases of Addison's disease. Addison's is a disease of the endocrine system. It is also called adrenal insufficiency. No one can live without the glands of the endocrine system, which include the pituitary, thyroid, pancreas, and adrenals. All these glands have life-giving hormones. The adrenal glands are the size of walnuts, sit on the kidneys, and produce aldosterone and corticosterone. These are called adrenal-cortex steroids, and are imperative in protein and carbohydrate metabolism. (As you can tell, I have read a lot about adrenal glands since Barbara became ill.) The Psalmist tells us that "I will give thanks to You, for I am fearfully and wonderfully made;" (139:14). My adrenal glands have been working away, producing hormones all these years, and I didn't even know they were there, let alone know what they did! I learned a lot about the endocrine system in a very short time.

Barbara's tests proved to be very abnormal, so she was sent by ambulance to the Children's Hospital of Southwestern Ontario in London. There she was placed in the care of a pediatric endocrinologist, whose specialty is the endocrine system in children. He confirmed the diagnosis that she had Addison's disease. Barbara was 14 years old, and she weighed 68 pounds. Once she was stabilized on medication, the doctor revealed the extent of Barbara's condition. The truth was, he told us, that she might possibly have lived only about three more weeks.

God had intervened in Barbara's life. He had brought Dr. Beatty across my path at just the right time. I am convinced that He gave her the desire to befriend me. Many doctors have never seen a case of Addison's. It is considered a middle-aged man's disease and is quite rare. In children and especially girls, it is almost unheard of, yet here was a doctor who had dealt with it and recognized the symptoms.

God was about to intervene again, and this time it came in the form of a phone call. Barbara needed daily medication to stay alive now, just as a diabetic does. She required cortisone to replace the cortisol the adrenals were no longer producing, and florineff to keep her kidneys functioning. I had no benefit package where I worked, so I had no idea how I would possibly afford her monthly prescriptions. When Barara was discharged from the hospital the doctor gave me a ninety-day supply of her medication. I claimed God's promise that He has made to us in Philippians 4:19 that He would supply all our need, and just left it there, not knowing how He would do this.

Again the phone rang one night, and it was another woman I knew through my political involvements. She had heard about Barbara's illness and knew that I had no benefits. She was a board member for the local Housing Authority, and knew of a job opening coming up that would offer me a full benefit package, including drug coverage. She arranged a job interview for me.

Audrey, the Housing Authority manager, did the interview. I knew if I had to have a typing test, I was in deep trouble. Even after working for a year, I still had not learned to type very well. She had been told about my daughter's illness and began by asking questions about her. Her fascination with Addison's disease came about because she was reading a book and the central character had the same disease. God must smile when He makes us smile. Inside, I was actually chuckling because I knew this was no coincidence.

Audrey hired me without a typing test, and before Barbara's medications ran out, I had full benefits and never had to pay for her prescriptions. I want to tell you that you can be absolutely confident that God will keep His Word and meet your need.

In the devotional book that I am reading today, *The Power of His Presence* (based on the writings of Ray Steadman), the author says if you want to live to please God, "you have the full authority of the throne of God behind you; you may proceed with full confidence that the unseen, but real, power of God is backing you up" (2006, p. 245). Over and over again, God has proven His power and faithfulness in my life in these situations that for me were humanly impossible to work out. God is always there in that space between us and our need.

The years I worked at the Housing Authority were eventful in my personal life as well as at work. It was during this time that I moved out of the house and rented an apartment for Barbara and me, since the boys had moved to their own places, and they were no longer my responsibility. Becoming the breadwinner and working mom was a new challenge in my life. My one constant was the church. I continued to teach in the young people's Sunday school department at Temple Baptist Church and attend a weekly Bible study. That source of stability in my uncertain world was something for which I was very thankful. I had also begun to teach one-on-one and passed along to many women the wonderful truths from the Scriptures that Lois had taught me which had changed my life.

As I look back, I am pleased to see that I never tried to hide the fact at work that I was a Christian, and the Lord used that. I used to sing at my typewriter, so I could have victory over how much I disliked it. I had learned that what I allowed to stay in my mind had a definite impact on my emotions. If I kept hymns in my mind, I didn't mind the typing so much and did a far better job at it. Isaiah tells us this same truth, that what is in your mind affects your feelings. "The steadfast of mind You will keep in perfect peace, Because he trusts in You" (Isaiah 26:3).

Audrey, the Housing Authority manager, was suffering from very high blood pressure. Many times she fainted or was ill, and one of our staff would have to call an ambulance to take her to the hospital. The doctors kept telling her she would have a stroke if she didn't quit working and quit smoking. I would just keep telling her that I was praying for her.

One day she called me into her office and began questioning me about the Bible. I tried to answer her questions and ended up presenting the Gospel to her. How it happened was quite amazing. She had not closed any of the doors to her office, and usually people were coming and going. I prayed and asked God to keep everybody away, so I could share with her. That day, everyone came back late from lunch. I ended up praying with her, and she received Christ right there at her desk. I was elated. It was only a few months later, that at 53 years old, Audrey would die of an aneurysm. I thank God that I know I will see her one day when I go home to be with Him.

Another girl in the office seemed to have everything, a great husband who loved her, a lovely daughter, health, a smart mind, lots of money, and a beautiful home. We became very friendly, and I was invited many times to her home for lunch and swimming. Her backyard was wonderful with a full-sized pool. I looked at people like her and thought how can you possibly share Christ with them because they have everything and seem to have no need of God? But I was wrong, and soon, she shared that her life seemed empty, and all that she had brought her no satisfaction. She couldn't get over the fact that I seemed to have nothing but struggles, yet she saw in me a peace and joy that she knew she didn't have.

One day at the office, she came and asked me about my faith, and what I believed. I told her all about my experience of receiving Christ as my Savior, and what God had done for me since. She didn't respond to me then, but the next time she came into work, she was beaming.

She had gone home and thought about what I had said, and asked Christ to save her. I haven't thought about some of these experiences in years, but praise God He has not forgotten any of them. Remembering, I truly thank God for the blessed life I have had in the years since I've come to know Him.

During those years at the Housing Authority, I was meeting with Monica every week. She was a gifted listener. I talked constantly about the struggle of adjusting to working, coping with Barbara's illness, and my struggles with loneliness. Victory over self-pity was work. I had to keep clinging to what I had learned during my years with Lois.

In remembering those days, I can see now that Monica was truly a gift from the Lord. It was her listening to me as I poured out my heart to her that helped to bring emotional healing in my life. In talking to her about this time, she has always said that she really didn't do anything, and that it was while I was talking my way through my situations that God did His work in my heart. Many different people came and went in my life. Some brought encouragement, and the maturing of my faith, but there were also some, through criticism of the decisions I had made, that caused me to struggle with discouragement. But I am convinced that all was orchestrated by God in order to complete His work in me.

Ephesians 6:10–12 tells us:

> *Finally, be strong in the Lord and in the strength of His might. Put on the full armor of God, so that you may be able to stand firm against the schemes of the devil. For our struggle is not against flesh and blood, but against the rulers, against the powers, against the world forces of this darkness, against the spiritual forces of wickedness in the heavenly places.*

I put this verse in here because I want it understood that the Apostle Paul is trying to tell us that we need the armour for our war with Satan. We are not in a war with people. Many times we see the people in our lives as the enemy, but it is Satan who is the enemy, and only using the people as tools to try to defeat us in our walk with God.

Some of the paths that I have walked have been the consequences of the choices I have made, but other times, for instance, my husband's infidelity, was not my choice. I never chose to be single. I assumed my marriage would be for life. I am thankful for the Scripture that records the Apostle Paul's struggle on his path. In this record, there are no daily, moment-by-moment descriptions, yet according to the written record he struggled as we do. We see a glimpse of his struggle in Romans 7. It is the same one that we go through on a daily basis in this journey God has placed before us. In giving us a picture of his struggles in the flesh, Paul makes sure that he ends with thanks to God for victory in Christ (Romans 7:25). Paul's record in the Scriptures does not glorify his sin and failure, but the things recorded are for God's glory. I have had many failures in this walk, but also many victories, and as the Apostle's purpose was to glorify the Lord, I too want that to be the purpose of these writings.

The purpose here also, is that in sharing my victory that you might be encouraged in your walk with Christ. My gift is exhortation, and my heart's desire is to exhort you to walk worthy of your calling, get into the Word of God, and put your trust in Him so that you will strengthen your confidence in Him.

Those years of working at the Housing Authority (1981–1988), from today's vantage point seem to have moved along quickly. I have discovered it is only in looking back that you can really see God working all things for good in your life as He promises in Romans 8:28. Sometimes in the present it is not real to you that what you are going through is really good for you.

There is a picture here that comes to my mind as I am writing; it is of you and I trudging along through my story, and we have just sat down to have a little chat, but now it is time to start walking again. Just around the corner there is a new adventure.

NINE
Impossible Dreams

1 988 came and the passage of time brought a stability and routine in
my life. I was living in an apartment and working fulltime. Barbara
had been left with some physical disabilities because of her disease. She
had started receiving her own pension including a benefit package that
covered the cost of her drugs, but she still lived with me. Through the
years of upheaval, the Lord had been developing in me a sense of security
in Him that I had never known before. I was learning the reality of His
love and care. During this growth process, the desire had arisen to know
God deeper and also a desire to really know His Word.

While visiting a friend one day, our discussion came around to the
subject of what we would really like to be doing, and she shared that her
heart was really in missions. I told her about how I wanted to study the
Bible full-time. We laughed because for both of us, these were impossible dreams.

April rolled around, and it was time for the annual Missions Conference at the church. That year the theme was "To the Glory of God." My
friend and I went almost every night. Both of us had been deeply
touched by the messages, which had focused on the truth that the real
purpose of our lives is that they may bring God glory. Solomon also came
to this conclusion at the end of Ecclesiastes where he writes, "The conclu-

sion, when all has been heard, is: fear God and keep His commandments, because this applies to every person" (Ecclesiastes 12:13).

Coming home from the conference that evening, and sorry that it was drawing to a close, I got on my knees by my bed and told the Lord that all I wanted for the rest of my days was that somehow He would be glorified in my life. How this would happen I had no idea.

The last evening of the conference came to an end, and the pastor who had been the main speaker gave an invitation to all who had felt touched that week by the Lord to come forward to commit themselves full-time to God. With tears pouring down our faces, my friend and I went forward. Several others had also come, and the pastor took us into another room to speak individually to each of us.

My turn came to speak with him, and he asked me why I had come forward, and out of my mouth came words that I had not really thought about. I said, "I want to go to Bible college full-time." I really felt as if someone else had said it. He said "great!" But I told him that was impossible and explained my situation. I was self-supporting, with no money except a bi-weekly paycheck, and some responsibility for Barbara. He simply replied, "If this is what God wants you to do, He will meet all your needs to do it."

Sitting in my friend's car in the driveway of my apartment building, I felt like a complete fool. My friend did too. She had declared that her heart was in missions, and all she wanted to do was tell the little children about Jesus. That was not possible for her as she was married to an unsaved man with children still at home. We could see that we were dreaming impossible dreams.

Jeremiah writes to us, "Thus says the Lord who made the earth, the Lord who formed it to establish it, the Lord is His name, 'Call unto me and I will answer you, and I will tell you great and mighty things, which you do not know'" (Jeremiah 33:2–3). That is what God wants to do in our lives, in spiritual and supernatural ways that the world does not recognize, and ways that we sometimes cannot understand.

Proverbs 3:5–7 tells us

> *Trust in the Lord with all your heart And do not lean on your own understanding. In all your ways acknowledge Him, And He will make your paths straight. Do not be wise in your own eyes; Fear the Lord and turn away from evil.*

There it is in the Scriptures for all of us to read: that God does things, allows things, and works in ways that we cannot understand at the time. Sometimes He reveals His purpose later on, but sometimes only eternity will show His plans. God wanted me to go to Bible College. I felt certain about it, yet the impossibility of it loomed before me.

The Apostle Paul wrote to the Corinthians, "For the love of Christ controls us" (2 Corinthians 5:14). Webster's defines control to mean "power or authority to guide or manage" (1987, p. 285). It is difficult to put into words how I felt about going to Bible College, but Paul's word "controls" in that context fits very well. It was so absurd to think that God would want a 49-year-old grandmother to go to school full-time; I did have a lot of difficulty with it. I talked to Lois and asked for prayer. I talked to Monica and asked for prayer. They were both excited and encouraging.

As I think about those days, I remember them as an emotionally confusing time, with encouragement from some, discouragement from others. My family was not overly supportive, although they did not try to discourage me. The one really bright spot was my Bible study teacher at the church. She was very enthusiastic about the idea, and really encouraged me to take the steps necessary to apply to school and leave it with the Lord to open a door or block the way.

Today, faced with the prospect of writing this book, I feel like I am in a similar situation. I am an ordinary person, in my tiny corner of the world, and know nothing of writing a book. It is just another impossible dream. But because of God's miraculous working in my life twenty years ago, I have learned that I can believe Him today. Although I do not always understand what He is doing, I can leave the results of my obedience with Him, and just continue to be an instrument in His hands for His purpose. Thanks be to God.

The application from the Bible college came in the mail. It required personal information, references, and my handwritten testimony. Putting things on paper has always been hard for me. I'm not even good at writing letters, so filling out the application and writing my testimony was a daunting task. I was filled with fear of humiliation and failure. What if they didn't accept me? What if they laughed at my testimony? The papers lay on the table for a few days while my doubts assailed me. It really was such a foolish idea for me to think that God would want me to do this. God had to convince me that the idea was His not mine.

It took several days of struggling emotionally with this, but finally I sat down and filled in all the personal information required, as well as the references. But as I began to write out my testimony, paralyzing fear got a grip on me, and I couldn't seem to make myself do it. Dropping to my knees, I prayed, "Lord if this is truly from You and this is Your will; please show me very specifically so I can know this is what You want me to do."

That evening while I was sitting on the couch with the application in front of me, the telephone rang. It was Dr. Beatty, the doctor who had saved Barbara's life. She was now living in London, Ontario. Since I had done some dog sitting for her in the past, she wanted to know if I could dog sit for her again.

Just making conversation she asked, "What were you doing?"

"You'll never believe this," I replied. "I'm filling out an application for London Baptist Bible College."

"That's great news." she said, "Where are you going to stay?"

"I don't know," I told her. "I haven't even thought that far ahead yet." Thank God that He had planned ahead of me in answer to my prayer.

Dr. Beatty shared that a friend of hers had called her with a prayer request from the Bible college. They desired that a mature female student would come to the school that year. There was an elderly lady in London who lived alone, and who had called the school to offer free room and board to a mature female student in exchange for light house-keeping and preparing some food for her. Isaiah 65:24 says, "It will also come to pass that before they call, I will answer; and while they are still speaking, I will hear." God had very specifically answered my prayer before I asked. I had needed convincing that this dream of Bible college was something that God had given to me and not just some harebrained idea of mine. With Dr. Beatty's phone call, I began to be very excited about the prospect that this could really happen.

By the end of that evening, I had finished writing my testimony and the application was in the envelope ready for the mail. By this time it was into the month of June, and I was very late to be sending in an application to College. I mailed it with a prayer for acceptance according to God's plan. I asked God to intervene that I might hear from the school quickly, as I needed to give notice at work if I was to leave my job by the end of August.

One week later, I received my acceptance letter. One week! It still causes me to stand in awe of our God when I think of how many times He has miraculously moved in my life. I called the woman in London, and talked to her, and accepted her offer of free room and board for my whole year. I was actually on my way to Bible College. With God directing our steps, there is no end to new beginnings.

TEN
School Days...Help!!

L abour Day weekend 1988 came quickly; Barbara's friend moved in with her, and I went off to London. I had left behind family, job, paycheck and benefit package, and stepped out in faith, absolutely convinced that God had orchestrated all this. I laugh when I tell people that this is a different story than most, in that I was the mom who left home and went to school not the other way around. I had applied for some Ontario Student Assistance Program loans (a Canadian Government Program for post-secondary students), but had not received any confirmation from the government, so when I arrived at the school, I had no idea how I was financially going to do this. I had one paycheck in the bank, and faith that God would do it. When I told this to the school secretary, she simply said, "It has been taken care of." The money for the year had already arrived at the school before me.

There I was at school with all the details worked out. From the missions conference in April, until I was standing at the school was only four short months. It was amazing. 1 Thessalonians 5:24 says, "Faithful is He who calls you, and He also will bring it to pass." The Scriptures tell us that God is the potter and we are the clay (Romans 9: 20–21), and it is the potter who supplies everything the clay needs to be the finished work the potter desires. I lacked nothing to be where the Lord wanted me to be.

The syllabus is the course requirements given to each student at the beginning of the semester. I received one for each subject I took. I don't know how to describe the terror that assailed me at the end of the first week of school after I had looked at all the course requirements for my first semester. I was trying to hold on to everything I had learned spiritually, but the old fear of failure almost swamped me.

The day I turned sixteen years old, I dropped out of high school not even completing grade 10, and except for a few typing courses I had not been in school since. Now here I was at the college level. Inside I was screaming, "HELP!! Do I even know what a research paper is? Do the professors really expect me to do all this? What have I done? Please God, help me!"

Only in the place where we feel uncomfortable, weak and insecure in ourselves are we pliable in the hand of God. It is in these places where we cry out to Him that He does His work to change us into the image of His Son, and He can truly use us as an instrument in His mighty hands. It was an uncomfortable place to which I had come. I was enrolled in a Bible college at 49 years old with no understanding as to how this level of education operated. I can not remember another time when I felt so scared and so helpless. Looking at the course requirements, I knew that I needed help.

God gave me the courage to share with some of the seminary students my worst fears. They would gather in a place called "The Oasis." It was a large comfortable room filled with couches and stuffed chairs. When I shared my struggles, they completely understood how I was feeling, and helped me to realize that I just needed to do a semester calendar. They patiently explained how I should put down on my calendar daily and weekly due dates for projects and reading schedules.

They helped me to see that I needed to take one thing at a time as it came due, complete it, and go to the next. This huge mountain that I was facing now became a realistic hill. Whew!! I began to think I might just live through this whole experience.

Classes were very enjoyable for me; I particularly loved the lectures. I was hearing things about the Bible I had not known, and I felt like a sponge soaking up all this new information. I usually sat near the front of the class and asked a lot of questions. There seemed to be no end to my hunger to know more about the Scriptures. I was trying to learn new study habits while preparing for tests, knowing that at the middle and end of the semester I would be facing exams. I didn't allow myself to think about that too much, or I probably would have just packed up and gone home.

One of my first semester courses was the study of the book of Genesis. I loved it. The history is amazing, and seeing God's great hand working out His salvation for the people of Israel was exciting. Most of my study since becoming a Christian had been in the New Testament. I had read and heard a lot of Old Testament stories, but to actually study a book in-depth and learn all the background information was new for me. I was drinking in all the professor had to offer. I came down off my cloud with a heavy thump when I discovered I was required to write a ten page paper on a single verse in Genesis.

The course outline stated that a research paper for Genesis was required, that it must be ten pages, researching one verse, pros and cons, with bibliography and footnotes. I started by going to the dictionary to find out what the syllabus meant by bibliography and footnotes. One of my prayers in the previous few years had been that God would make my security in Him real to me. I had never envisioned this place when I had contemplated His answer to that prayer. But that is exactly what He was doing.

After I had walked the floor, wringing my hands, praying and crying, I went back to "The Oasis," and again asked for help. The seminary students explained step-by-step how to research a subject, make notes of all the references, and how to put it together. I was referred to a woman who would type it up for me. The verse I chose was Genesis 3:16. Bathed by a lot of prayer, I took it step-by-step just as I was told to do. After gathering all my research, I sat down and wrote my paper. I sent it off to the typist before I could change my mind, and when it came back, too afraid to even read it over, I turned it in to the professor.

God makes us so many wonderful promises in His Word that we can lean on. Why is it so hard for us to trust Him? Philippians 4:13 says, "I can do all things through Him who strengthens me" yet in these situations out of our comfort zone, it is hard to get hold of that. I was just living day-by-day believing God to meet my needs, claiming His promises, and thanking Him for what He was doing. Slowly as I worked my way through the semester, faced exams, and completed projects, I could see that He was doing just what He said He would. By the way, I got 97 per cent on my Genesis paper. It turned out to be the highest mark in the class. Praise God! I made it through one semester!

Christmas vacation came, and I might add, not a day too soon for me. I had developed a bad cold and by New Years it had turned into pneumonia. I ended up missing the first week of the new semester. By the end of January, I was back into the school routine working on projects, one at a time. Then one evening the phone rang.

Tom was calling to tell me he wanted a divorce. He would take care of everything, including the legal costs, and all I had to do was sign the papers. It had been eight and a half years since we separated. I was devastated. It was as if our 25 years together and six children meant nothing at all. I had been praying daily for his salvation, but now our marriage was to come to an end.

Infidelity and marriage failure is a deep emotional valley to get through. It robbed me of any sense of value I had about my life. The fact that both my father and my husband had rejected me was a hard truth. I tried to hold on to the truth that I knew that God would never leave me nor reject me. It is so hard to keep believing God for answered prayer when circumstances around you can be so difficult. To keep having faith in what you don't see, and ignore what is so real in our humanity is hard work. God once again had to remind me of that familiar verse of Proverbs 3:5: "Trust in the Lord with all your heart And do not lean on your own understanding."

When I had enrolled in Bible College it had been with a missions minor, but I could not stay in a mission's course if I was divorced. I had to switch to the counseling minor instead. At the time, I had no idea why this was happening. Over and over again, I had to stop myself from trying to figure this out and practice praising the Lord. "Thank you Lord for what you are doing in all this!" I repeated that prayer again and again. 1 Thessalonians 5:18 says, "in everything give thanks;" This verse does not tell me I have to feel thankful; it simply says "give thanks." John 3:16 says, "For God so loved the world, that He gave His only begotten Son." Gave is a verb. It is an action word. I don't have to feel anything; I just have to do something. I had to get back to the present job of continuing my studies.

One of the topics in my counseling course was dealing with how you handle a situation when someone has hurt you. The professor said that we should pray about it, and then go to that person and confront them in a loving manner. He or she needs to be told that we have been hurt. My problem was that the person in my life who had hurt me most was already dead. So I posed the question to my professor, "what do I do about this?" This was his answer: "You sit the person on a chair and tell them how they hurt you." I went to my apartment, locked the door and pulled the blinds, so no one could see me or hear me. If I was going to sit my father on a chair, I did not want anyone to know. They would think I was crazy. I put a chair in the middle of the floor, and sat down and began to talk as if my father were sitting there.

At first it was uncomfortable, but as memories began to come back, and I remembered some of the things that had really hurt me, I began to cry, and discovered I was able to pour out some things that had been long buried. It was very therapeutic. I also realized that I had completely forgiven him. I had no bitterness toward him. Then I picked up my Bible, flipped it open, and asked the Lord for encouragement from His Word. I had turned to Jeremiah 31:3, and the verse I read was, "I have loved you with an everlasting love; Therefore I have drawn you with lovingkindness." The wonderful truth of that verse hit me: my heavenly FATHER loves me. I believed that God loved me, and gave His Son for me, but it was the first time for me that God's love was a genuine experience. Now, I absolutely knew it. God was causing me to understand that I was neither unloved nor rejected. Praise Him!

The winter semester passed quickly until there were only about two weeks to go until the end of the school year. I was exhausted and so glad that it was coming to a close. One day I was sitting in "The Oasis" chatting with the seminary students when they asked me if I was coming back in September. "Absolutely not," I replied in a hurry. "I have had enough of school, thank you very much!" They all said, "Oh, that's too bad. You should really come back. You did great this year." My answer was a resounding "No!"

The day following this chat with the young men in "The Oasis," we were having a special chapel service to finish off our year before final exams began. I don't remember who the speaker was, but will never forget the message that hit me. "Are you willing to give all of your life to the Lord? Will you go anywhere and do anything He wants you to do?" I was so convicted. I had willingly left my job, and came to school for the sole purpose that God would be glorified in my life. Did He really want me to continue? The speaker asked the question, "does God want you to continue in school?" and into my mind popped the verse about God's faithfulness. "Faithful is He who calls you, and He also will bring it to pass" (1 Thessalonians 5:24). I went forward at that chapel service to say "yes" to God. Facing three more years of school, I realized I would be 53 years old at graduation.

God in His grace supernaturally intervened on my behalf during my college years, and in some amazing ways, met my need. One of these ways was financially.

Prayers for my living accommodations were continuously answered by God. My first year was free room and board; my second was a beautiful home that I shared with three other female students from the college and paid $100.00 per month, including cable TV, utilities, and regular monthly phone bills. Any long distance calls were paid individually. It was a miracle. In my third year, the school offered me a job as the Resident Director in the girls' dorm. I lived with the female students, had my own apartment and the school covered all my living costs. It was another miracle. My student loan money covered tuition and books.

Cash flow was always a difficulty. I had no benefits, so that meant all my personal hygiene and cleaning products, and prescriptions came out of my pocket money. The school had a dress code then, and so I always had to have dress clothes, shoes and pantyhose. Financially, things could get very tight at times. But God was faithful. Philippians 4:19 promises that He will meet our needs, and He always did that. My purse and pockets would be empty, and I would go to my mailbox and there would be an envelope with money. Someone supported me throughout my school years and faithfully sent me money weekly. I believe that God moves people so that these things are done anonymously, and then He alone will receive the glory and thanks.

There was another time that I was desperate. I had become very good friends with one of the seminary students and his wife and family. Jim was doing part-time classes to get his Bachelor of Theology degree required to be an ordained pastor. His wife worked part-time as a nurse. They had five children. The more I got to know them, the more I could see what a financial struggle school was for them. But they simply believed it was God's plan for them and continued in this belief.

One day I had been crying on my knees because I was out of food and had no money, when someone knocked on my door. It was Jim's wife with $150.00 for me. I felt I couldn't accept this money from her because of their struggles, but she told me about her prayer for me, and that God had answered in this way. They had also needed money and she prayed that God would supply with $300.00, so that she could help me and give me half. Someone put an envelope in her mailbox with the $300.00 in it, and she was at my door with my half. How do you begin to say thanks for these supernatural miracles of God's grace on your behalf?

Neither time nor pages will allow me to write about all the prayers answered and all the needs met in the time I was in school. But the one thing that I can write about with complete confidence is God's overwhelming faithfulness in this endeavor which He called me to. I had taken a giant step of faith in going to school, and I believe God honored that faith with His absolute faithfulness to me. This experience contributed to teaching me to really believe the Word of God.

In the spring of my third year, my time as Resident Director in the women's dorm came to an end, and I had to move out of my apartment. With almost no money, and only a part-time job, I asked for much prayer and kept this need before the Lord.

Turner's Drugstore was one block from the school, and almost directly across the street from the dormitory. At the time I didn't know that Turner's owned the house next door. It was an old, late nineteenth century home that had been made into five apartments. I had become friends with one of the ladies who worked at the store, who was a Christian, and in asking her for prayer, found out that one of the apartments was going to be vacant. It was a very small one bedroom, but the $300.00 per month rent, including utilities, convinced me that God's leading was involved. That was an unheard of rent in 1991, and it definitely got my attention. I applied for and got the apartment, and as an added blessing, the rent was reduced to $250.00 if I would keep the entranceway and stairwell cleaned and vacuumed. To add to my blessings, I got a part-time position at the drugstore. Again, God had kept His Word.

Settling into my new apartment, I realized I was facing my final year in school. I had successfully completd three years of college, but I would be 53 years old, divorced, and penniless at graduation. My first thought was, "What possible purpose could God have for me in all of this? Why Lord? What is going on? Why is this happening? Do you really have a purpose in all of this?" I know that I am not alone in my desire to know why. I believe it is a part of every Christian's walk to want to know why God is working the way He is.

Proverbs tells us that we are not to try to understand what God is doing (Proverbs. 3:5). We are but to trust Him, that He will direct our path. Isaiah 55:8–9 gives the same message to us,

> *For My thoughts are not your thoughts, Nor are your ways My ways, declares the Lord. For as the heavens are higher than the earth, So are My ways higher than your ways and My thoughts higher than your thoughts.*

Then verse 10 tells us how absurd we are to try to fathom His ways and doings, even in our own lives. Neither can we come up with an answer to the question why. Sometimes out of His love and compassion for us He shows us an answer, but sometimes He never does. God simply wants us to trust Him and be thankful.

No major events or calamities assailed me that final semester. God had done it, had brought me through Bible College, but upon finishing my final exams, I realized "Help, Lord, I need a job." God was about to open an amazing door.

God's ultimate work in our lives is to change us into the image of His Son, so that He might become the firstborn of "MANY" brethren (Romans 8:29). For each of us, it is a different work. He leads us along our personal paths which will work to make us Christ like. I believed that post-secondary education was a pathway to a career, so with much anticipation, I looked forward to finding out why God had me struggle through college at my age. I would find out eventually.

ELEVEN
More Beginnings

It was just an ordinary Sunday morning when I met someone whom God would use to start me in a new and very different ministry from what I had yet experienced. Every Sunday, when the morning worship service at church was over, we would congregate in the foyer for visiting. I always laugh and tell my daughter that anyone watching and listening to this weekly ritual would think that these people had not seen each other for years and had a lot of catching up to do. But it was such an enjoyable time. Everyone stood around and gabbed up a storm. One of the rich blessings of being part of the body of Christ is this true enjoyment and oneness that we have with our brothers and sisters.

While I stood talking that Sunday, out of the corner of my eye I caught sight of a man I had never seen at church before. I went over, and after introducing myself, invited him to come along with some of us for a coffee.

In the conversation at the coffee shop, we found out that John had been saved through difficult circumstances. He had recently been arrested and jailed; now out on bail, but not being able to go home, he was staying at the Salvation Army men's hostel. It was there that one of the officers had shared the Gospel with him and led John to the Lord. John was a terribly frightened man who knew he would have to serve a jail term, but it was that fear of what he faced that brought Him to Christ, so John praised the Lord for the situation that God used to save him.

This all happened at the end of my final semester at school. I went to court with John, and when he was sentenced to two years less a day, I began visiting him at the London jail. He soon discovered that his cellmate was also a Christian. Because the rules were two visits per week, and because the inmates could make only collect phone calls, I would accept John's calls, and talk to him and his roommate on days when they couldn't have visits. During these weeks, I was learning new things about the incarceration system that I had never known before.

There are local detention centres that are for inmates waiting for court trials, court sentencing, or those serving 30, 60, or 90 days, and they also accommodate those people who are doing their sentences on weekends. Then there are provincial jails for anyone serving up to two years, less one day. The federal penitentiary system is for all those sentenced to more than two years. The London jail is a maximum security jail, and referred to as a detention centre as it detains federal inmates as well as provincial. I had no idea what the Lord would do with all this newfound knowledge of mine and certainly no idea how my graduating from Bible college would fit into it. I did graduate, and believed that God had a specific purpose in all this, but where would it all lead? At the moment only God knew.

With no more studies, and only part-time work, I started to watch the noon news on the local TV station. Part of their service to the community was to offer a daily list of employers with job placements. It was about three weeks after I finished school, that a job opportunity jumped off the TV screen at me. The Salvation Army wanted someone with counseling training at their men's hostel. I found out where it was, rushed over there, and dropped off my resume. They were very kind, thanked me very much, and said they would be in touch. I just prayed over and over all the way home, "fit me into your plans Lord." Two days later I received a phone call to arrange an appointment for an interview.

On the world's list of greatest stressors, right up there with death and divorce, is an employment interview. It is one of the most difficult situations that life has to offer. I am so glad that the Apostle Paul wrote so honestly about his struggle with fear in 1 Corinthians 2:3, "I was with you in weakness and in fear and in much trembling," So with trembling and trusting, I went to my job interview.

As with most things we fear, the fear is usually worse than the reality of the situation. The interview went well, and to my surprise and joy part of the job would be working with federal inmates at the halfway house, as well as the homeless men that came and went at the hostel. The next day, I received a call that I had been accepted for the job. I was ecstatic.

Ephesians 2:10 explains to us that we were created in Christ Jesus for good works, "which God prepared beforehand so that we would walk in them." To my surprise and delight my job contributed to developing in me a love for working with inmates in the correctional system. In all the years leading up to working for the Salvation Army, I had never even really thought about prisoners or transients, so how much I loved my job was all of the Lord's doing. I was never offended by the Hostel residents or the inmates, their lack of hygiene or by their choice of language.

As I started my new job at the hostel, I found residing there an assortment of alcoholics, drug addicts, thieves, and even murderers. Please don't think I see myself as some super saint. I don't mean to imply that. I was remembering how burdened I was for missions when I first went to school, and now I could see that God had placed me in the middle of a mission field right there in London, Ontario. Not only had I ended up in "missions," but also the counseling training I received was what I would really need to be used at the hostel and at the jail. God blessed me with the ability to see these men with His eyes, to recognize that they were created in His image, that they were loved by Him, and that Jesus had died for them. You see, this was not my harebrained idea at all, and I was fully convinced.

The hostel was located in an area of London that was close to the downtown core. There were some small industries around, a few stores, and Labatt's Breweries (it seemed an irony with a good portion of the residents struggling with alcoholism). A thrift store and donation distribution centre was connected to the hostel in a large rambling building that was built in the early fifties by the Salvation Army. I especially enjoyed the store as part of where I worked because I got to shop on all my coffee breaks and lunch hours.

The upper two stories of the hostel housed four large dorm rooms full of single beds, a number of private rooms, shower and washroom facilities. Also housed on the third floor was the halfway house for federal inmates on parole. On the main floor were the management offices, the main reception area, a chapel, a staff lounge, and my office. Down in the basement was the kitchen, dining room, and food storage areas. We could accommodate ninety men per night, and usually served around a hundred men three meals a day. We provided four large holiday meals a year, Easter, Thanksgiving, Christmas, and New Years. These special meals sometimes served three hundred, and beside the residents, they were open to all men and families of low income status.

My job included receptionist duties, and liaison with the Social Services Network, including welfare, disability, and pensions for the residents. I was also working with the detention centre, parole officers, addiction facilities, and the detoxification centre. I was challenged and fascinated with my job. The only slight drawback was the pay. I started at $7.10 an hour. I was still praising God for my low-rent apartment.

Going to the jail twice a week to visit John and his cellmate Ron had become a regular routine for me. So it was only natural that when some of our clientele went to jail, if they had no one to visit them, I would go and see them. Most of them didn't have anyone because of their lifestyles. Many of them had long ago been abandoned by family and friends. They had no idea what it was like to feel loved. But one thing I was sure of was that God loved them, and Jesus had died for them. So, I would go for a half hour visit once or twice a week in the public visiting area. It consisted of a long room, with large windows. At each window was a visitor's place that had a stool and telephone on the wall. This is the maximum security style of visiting. The inmates come into the room on the other side of the glass, and they also have a telephone and a stool to sit on.

Letting my mind go back to those days renews some wonderful memories, but it also causes some feelings of nostalgia. I cannot tell you how much I loved and enjoyed doing this visiting. Most of the inmates were very young, and so I was a motherly and grandmotherly image for them. All they wanted was someone to care and to listen to them. They loved the volunteers who would visit them.

Longing to be a registered volunteer visitor at the jail, I had applied to the chaplain to be considered. Unfortunately, she did not care for Evangelicals, so she denied me. So I just kept up my own visiting, always praying that God would open the door for me at the jail to be accepted as a volunteer. It would mean that I would not have to go into the public visiting room, but be allowed to go into the cellblocks where the inmates were housed. I needed a new miracle from God. It came quickly.

The process for visiting is not complicated, but I had to be prepared to wait, and I had to adhere to all the rules of the jail. I would approach a locked door, and speak into an intercom, and wait for someone inside to open the door. I would come into a sally port (the area between two locked doors), and wait for the door I came through to lock, and wait for the staff to unlock the inside door. I had to register my personal information at the desk and wait for permission to go into the visitor's area. When time was up, a Corrections Officer came and got the inmate and the visit was over.

On an ordinary Friday evening, when my visit with John and Ron was over, I came out of the visiting area and back to the desk to sign out. A female officer was on duty and started talking to me. She asked me, "Do you have family in here because I see you are here every week?"

"No." I answered and proceeded to explain why I was visiting.

"You should apply to become a volunteer visitor," she said.

"I have tried," I replied, "but the chaplain won't accept me."

"You need to see the Volunteer Coordinator. She is the one in charge of volunteer visiting. I will give you her name and number, and you can give her a call."

The next day I called her, and within a week I had a tour of the jail cells, instruction on the visiting policy and rules, and had my picture taken for my ID tag. God does it in His way and in His time. Praise Him. I was in the jail as an accepted visitor. Now I could go on the days that fit my schedule, and the hours, and also go and visit one-on-one in the cell block, no more glass or telephones.

The Coordinator's name was Doreen, and we hit it off right from the start. It was as if I had known her forever. I still don't know why I am so amazed when God fits you into His plans, and that the fit is so right.

This began eleven years of jail ministry for me. I would pray and ask the Lord to guide Doreen in the selection of the right inmate of God's choosing for me to visit. I also continued to visit the hostel residents and halfway house residents who went to jail. Many of the men who are in federal halfway houses end up going back to jail. The joke at work became that I spent every weekend in jail. "What did you do on your weekend?" "Oh, I was in jail." Ha! Ha!

The full implication of what an amazing thing God had done for me did not really impact me until I spoke with Garrett Block who had started a successful jail ministry just outside of London, in Arva, Ontario called New Life Prison Ministry. The ministry does Bible studies by correspondence, mailing the inmate a study, and when it is finished, the inmate mails it back. Volunteers read them, correct them, and then mail out a new one. Garrett and I had talked on more than one occasion and discussed my working with them, but that never worked out.

He had tried to get into the London jail many times, but the chaplain blocked him and also prevented anyone visiting in the jail from their ministry. He said simply, "God has done this for you, and has a purpose for you, so stay as an independent visitor." As it was not the first miracle God had done for me, and would not be the last, I took his advice, and continued where God had placed me. It was so exciting to me to know that only God could have directed what happened.

During my time of visiting John's cellmate Ron, I found out that he had received a sentence of ten years to life and would be going to Kingston Penitentiary. All of his family had disowned him, and so he had no one to visit him. After Ron arrived in Kingston he continued to call me and write letters from Kingston, and asked if I would come to visit. This request would start another new chapter in my life.

TWELVE
Exciting Roads

Traveling is an enjoyable time for some people. Just getting in their cars and getting out on the highways is vacation to them. Not so with me. To me, the freeways are like race tracks where all the drivers think faster is better. Driving on them is another one of those places that would fall into the "out of my comfort zone" category. But my experience with the Lord over the years has been that He sees that category as one of the best for me. It stretches me and causes me to grow.

I felt compelled to visit Ron in Kingston. One problem for this to be accomplished was the fact that I did not have a car. So this matter had to come before the Lord in prayer. Fully convinced that God was motivating my desire to visit Ron, I simply laid all this out before the Lord, claiming His promises that if this was His will, He would supply all I needed to do it. The answer was not long in coming.

My son called me one day to say that he had seen a little car that would be perfect for me. He did not know about my prayers. I could not contain my excitement. We arranged to see it in Sarnia. The car was a small, four-door station wagon, sitting in a carport with four flat tires, but otherwise in good condition. After looking it all over, I told the owner that I would get back to him as soon as I could about purchasing it. Another small problem lay before me. He wanted $400.00 for it, and I didn't have any money, and no way of getting any. Jeremiah 33:3 says, "'Call to Me and I will answer you, and I will tell you great and mighty things, which you do not know.'" I smile to think how much the Lord loves what we perceive as insurmountable problems.

In the light of whom God is our prayers must seem very weak and feeble at times. I ask myself how many times I have prayed in doubt, not in faith. It was a Saturday that I saw the car, went home, and got on my knees and prayed, "Lord, if it really is your will for me to travel to Kingston, and You brought this car to my attention, I just ask You to meet my need for the $400.00 to pay for the car."

That Sunday after church, a man came over to me and pressed a paper into my hand. When I got outside and looked at what it was, it was a check for $400.00. Praise God. A song I have sung through the years is "My Father owns the cattle on a thousand hills, and the wealth in every mine." God is rich in every way, so $400.00 is nothing to Him. I always stood in awe when God did these miraculous things for me. It wasn't that I didn't believe He was able; it was that He did it for me. It was all of His choosing.

I was on my way to Kingston. I may be the only person that you will ever hear about that was happy to be on her way to prison. Now would begin the application process for visiting privileges at Kingston Penitentiary.

There are a few requirements for a federal prison application. I needed Ron to send me an application form. I had to have pictures taken. Two copies of my head shot were required. I had to supply two pieces of picture I.D. with the application. This process could take two to three weeks, and then the application is mailed to the institution, and you wait for a reply. The reply is either acceptance or rejection. I have learned that whenever I feel the Lord wanting me to do something, I just send it to Him, bathed in prayer, and leave Him to fit me into His plan.

If the Lord is not in it, it truly is a waste of time. God gifts us and designs the works for us that He wants us to do. "For we are His workmanship, created in Christ Jesus for good works, which God prepared beforehand so that we would walk in them" Ephesians 2:10 tells us. He alone knows where He wants us and what His plans are for each one of us individually. Over the years, I made many applications to visit in the federal penitentiary system.

God did a miraculous thing for me to prove I was doing what He wanted me to. The federal penitentiary system for all of Canada is governed by Corrections Canada, and their rules state that a person is allowed to visit only one inmate at a time in any of their federal institutions. Yet time and time again I was accepted as a visitor even when I was listed for several inmates at different institutions. I would honestly tell them I was on Ron's visiting list, and they would still approve me. It was nothing short of a miracle. God had opened a door in Kingston, just as He had in London.

A couple of weeks went by before I received my first acceptance as Ron's visitor, so now the arrangements for the trip would be made. My daughter Barbara was going with me for the first trip. I was nervous about the drive and just wanted the company.

Driving out of London on a Saturday morning, I thought our timing was pretty good, but that is not how it turned out because we got caught in the traffic in Toronto. What a first time harrowing experience that was. Have you ever been in five or six lanes of traffic, stuck in the far lane away from the exits, and your car starts to make a loud scary sound from one of the tires? Yes, that is exactly what happened.

Isaiah 41:10 popped into my mind. "Do not fear, for I am with you; Do not anxiously look about you, for I am your God".

In all situations, God had been teaching me how to trust Him, and this was another test to see if I would trust or fear. I was struggling with feeling very afraid, and I wanted to pull over, sit by the side of the road, and cry. Instead, I prayed and slowly worked my way over to the lane that would lead me to the nearest exit. I took it and found a Canadian Tire Store very close to the exit. A young man there checked my tires for me and found that one of the nuts had come loose and was rattling around inside my hubcap. That was the terrible noise which I heard. The tire was on tight with no fear of falling off, the young man told me, and it was just the awful noise the nut made in the metal hubcap that was the problem.

God wants us to learn to have peace in Him and not in our circumstances. Many things in this life will terrify us, but they are part of living in this world. God wants us to put our security in Him and not in our circumstances or feelings. The rest of the drive to Kingston was uneventful, and we arrived safely praising the Lord.

In remembering the days of prison ministry, I can see how fear ate at me and surrounded every visit and every trip. I visited several prisons, and made countless trips to Kingston and the surrounding area over eleven years, as I felt led by the Lord, yet I still struggled with fear over it.

One of the hardest lessons of being a Christian, and pleasing the Lord, is this difficulty of being obedient to the Word of God, in spite of our feelings. That is the crux of it. Standing on the Word of God, when all our emotions are pulling us in the opposite direction is an ongoing experience. As each new situation arises where we need to trust God,

Satan will shoot his fiery darts of fear and doubt our way. Today's lessons are hard to remember in tomorrow's new dilemma.

I can honestly say that in all my years of traveling, alone or with someone else, God never failed to provide. Many times circumstances arose that I did not understand, but they always worked out. On more than one occasion I rode with someone else instead of driving by myself. I was truly thankful as it was easier than going alone. One woman had a son who was in prison. She was a delightful Christian, whom I met through her son when he was at the London jail. She always drove to Kingston to visit him on his birthday, so we began traveling together. She had another son in Ajax, Ontario and I had friends there, so we would spend a night there coming and going. We had great fellowship on the road, which made the trip a blessing. When we would arrive in Kingston, I would drop her off for a day of visiting with her son, and she would let me take her car to go and do visiting at another institution. Praise God. I had company, no cost, and still did the visiting that God wanted me to do.

It was the same with another Christian woman whose husband was in prison. We would do day trips out of London, leaving at 3 a.m. and arriving in Kingston around 8 a.m. I would drop her off for the day and take her car to do other visiting. At 4 p.m. I would go back to meet her and have dinner with her and her husband. We would leave Kingston around 6 p.m. and arrive home at 11 p.m. It was an exhausting day, but blessed nonetheless. I had the incredible blessing of encouraging in the Lord inmates, who had been saved, as well as sharing Christ through giving my own testimony, or sharing the Word of God with many.

I am sure there are many times for all of us, that we believe we are doing what God wants us to do, things go very wrong, and we struggle to know why. One such time for me was on one of my Kingston trips. This incident happened after my car had to be taken off the road, and I no longer had a vehicle of my own. My Christian friend whose son was in prison, offered me her car to travel to Kingston for the weekend. I would visit her son as well as others. I was praising the Lord. I left London at my usual 3 a.m. The trip was uneventful until I arrived.

After spending the day visiting, I began looking for an inexpensive motel to stay the night. I was stopped at a red light. The light turned green so I proceeded into the intersection. Suddenly, a car on my left ran the red light and t-boned me. He crushed in the whole driver's side, but by the grace of God I wasn't hurt badly, only a bruised knee. I was shaken and sobbing when the other driver came over to me to see if I was okay. He was very concerned because I was crying so hard. But all I could stammer was, "this is not my car." I was very upset about my friend's car.

The police came, arranged for the car to be towed and took me to a motel. I called my friend in London to tell her. She was naturally upset about her car and needed to contact her insurance company. She called me back to let me know that the insurance company would arrange for the car to be towed, and would reimburse me for any costs that I incurred to travel back to London.

What was going on? That was my question directed to the Lord. I had thought He wanted me to make this trip. He had provided everything I needed, yet here I was in Kingston. I did not know a soul, had no way of doing any visiting, and with my friend's car disabled, I had to make some arrangement to get back home. I can smile as I write this now, but I was not smiling then. I was trying not to be afraid and trust the Lord. God reminded me of Isaiah 41:10 again.

As you can imagine I was praying very hard and asking God to work this all out. Thanking Him for what He was going to do, it came to my mind that Marg, my friend in London, had told me about a Christian family who were friends of her son on Wolfe Island just offshore near Kingston. I called her to see if someone could contact them for me, and I left the number where I could be reached. Very shortly, I received a call from this family, and soon they were on their way to pick me up.

God is so faithful, and it was, as I recall, an unforgettable weekend. They took me on the ferry to their home, treated me like one of the family, and made sure I got to all my prison visiting. Whatever plans they had for their weekend, they laid them aside to take care of me. They had four children and lived on a farm on the island. They gave me clothes, so I could trek around the barn with the kids. I trust God that I left them encouraged in relating all God had done for me in visiting the jail and prisons. We had such sweet fellowship together.

What a joy to be part of the family of God, that we can be put in situations that leave us with human strangers, yet they are as close as family when needed. Praise God! In Jesus' high priestly prayer in John 17, He prayed to the Father in verse 11, "That they may be one even as We are." Arrangements were made for me to take the Greyhound bus back to London. I was seated beside a woman who started up a conversation with me, and gave me the opportunity to relate all that had happened to me and in doing so got a wonderful chance to share the Lord with her. I arrived safely home, praising the Lord to all who would listen.

Many of my experiences were real blessings for me without the challenges. One such experience was with a female inmate. She had come to the London jail pregnant, having been transferred from another city. It is unusual for Corrections Canada to allow pregnant female inmates in the local jails.

There is a jail called the Yellow Brick House where pregnant female inmates are housed because they have all the maternity benefits required. The girl I began visiting in London had such a violent criminal record, that even though she was pregnant, the correctional authorities would not let her go the Yellow Brick House in order to protect the other inmates. I got very close to her.

She asked if I would go to the hospital and be with her during the birth of her baby, so I went to the volunteer co-coordinator and put in a request. She had to get permission from the commanding officer, but she also told me not to get my hopes up as they never usually did things like that. I wanted so much to be with this young lady because she had no family and no visitors. She also knew that they would immediately take her baby away from her, and she wouldn't even see it. So, I prayed and asked the Lord to intervene.

God answered my prayer in order to show this young woman His love, and I received permission to be with her. The jail called at 1:30 a.m. one morning to let me know that the ambulance was taking her to the hospital as she was in labor. I arrived to find her handcuffed by one hand to the bed in the maternity wing. I sat by her bed and held her other hand and just talked to her.

When the doctor arrived and she was about to deliver, he asked me to hold her hand and did not put me out of the room. I was there for the birth of her beautiful little girl. The baby was immediately taken away by Children's Aid, and within 24 hours, the mom was back in her cell in the jail.

It was a sad story, but I was truly blessed that God could use me to help this mom, and that this had never been allowed in the London jail before. The young woman was transferred back to her own city, and I did not see her again, nor did I ever hear how the baby was doing. That's the way it is with the prison system, but I will never forget my experience. What a privilege it is to be used by God to show His love for even those who seem the least deserving. God's Word tells us that He shows no partiality, when Peter said in Acts 10:34, "I most certainly understand now that God is not one to show partiality." God loves unconditionally, and equally.

During the years of living in London, working at the Salvation Army, and doing jail ministry, God was continuously working in me to change me. Different situations and experiences would reveal an area that needed attention. As I struggled through fear situations, finances, and health issues, God was there teaching me to let go of my independent spirit, and learn to lean on Him in every area of my life. I can relate to the Apostle Paul when he writes in Philippians 3:12, "Not that I have already obtained it or have already become perfect, but I press on so that I may lay hold of that for which also I was laid hold of by Christ Jesus." I was learning to press on, not to give up, letting God do the work in me that was necessary.

As a Christian, I have learned that school never really gets out. Oh, yes, there are a few vacations, in that sometimes things go along smoothly, but soon it is back to class, and we are in the process of learning again. As I look back at who I was when I started this new life with Christ, I can truthfully say with much joy, that I am no longer that person, that she is gone, and I am much happier with who I am today.

We are told in Philippians 3:13–14, "forgetting what lies behind and reaching forward to what lies ahead, I press on toward the goal for the prize of the upward call of God in Christ Jesus." We are to praise God and remember all He has done for us in Christ Jesus. We are admonished to look back and remember His death, burial and resurrection, but Paul reminds us that we are to put behind us our sin and failure, for when God forgives, He forgets. God is working throughout our lives to change us into the image of His son.

Today, I was reading chapter four in the gospel of Mark. The disciples were in the boat with Jesus, the terrible storm was upon them, and they were terrified, so they went to Him, and said to Him, "Teacher, do You not care that we are perishing?"(4:38). Jesus immediately calmed the storm, "And He said to them, "Why are you so afraid? Do you still have no faith?" (4:40). After all that God has done for me, all the victories I've experienced, I ask myself the same question, "Why am I so afraid? Have I no faith?" I believe from my own life experiences that our fear goes so deep that even we do not realize how it permeates every part of us. Look at the next verse in Mark: "Tthey became very much afraid" (4:41). Jesus had just spoken and calmed the storm, yet they were even more afraid than before.

In my past I have a record of failure, as I am sure we all have. I was a quitter. Fear of failure has paralyzed me in many circumstances, and I never recognized it for what it was. Only as the Lord has shown this to me, and I have confessed this fear and asked God to change me, have I truly been able to see how deeply this has affected me and every area of my life. I am reminded that I must keep practicing Philippians 3:13. I must keep putting my past failures behind me and looking ahead with my confidence in the Lord. Philippians 1:6 says, "For I am confident of this very thing, that He who began a good work in you will perfect it until the day of Christ Jesus."

Throughout the writing of this book, I have had many days when I just could not make myself sit down at the computer. As I come into the last few chapters, it is more and more difficult to sit down to write. I am so deeply convinced that God wants me to do this, yet it seems to me to be harder and harder.

Today as I read Mark chapter four again, I recognized that my fear of failure in finishing this is paralyzing. In the devotional book I am using, *The Power of His Presence*, (Pastor Ray Steadman's writings), the author writes, "Faith is the answer to fear" (p. 21). How easy it is to forget all that has gone before in God's dealings with us and let the immediate circumstances defeat us. A new day, a new challenge, and I am just as afraid as I was in the past.

THIRTEEN
Heartache & Sorrow

Every Christian knows the story of Job. In this story we are told that there is a righteous man, who pleases God, yet God allows Satan to have the opportunity to test him. We must remember that not only is something going on in Job's life, but we must look at what is going on in heaven at the same time. We are privy to the conversation between God and Satan. God is in control of this situation, and at no time is the control out of God's hands. He CHOOSES what happens, and puts stiff restrictions on Satan's behaviour. Job 5:7 tells us, "For man is born for trouble, As sparks fly upward." and in the gospel of John, Jesus tells us that "In the world you have tribulation" (John 16:33). None of us are strangers to trouble. It is how we handle it that shows how much we really love and trust God.

Sometimes our own choices bring trouble, but not always; sometimes, as we see in Job, it is a testing time sent from God. He must try us to prove and strengthen our faith. We must learn to become over comers, and only difficulty can train us. I had three years in a row where heartache and sorrow were my portion.

Day tripping is a fun thing to do on a weekend, because one can travel short distances, at minimal cost, still get things done at home, and be ready for work on Monday. My friend Matt and I loved to day trip.

One weekend in July in 1995, we went on a Saturday to St. Jacobs. It is a small Mennonite village just outside of Kitchener, Ontario. There are dozens of small stores displaying multiple choices of homemade wares. There is also a great restaurant to eat Mennonite cooking. My mouth is watering remembering the food, particularly the most delicious ice-cream made by the locals.

Arriving back in London at about 8 p.m. we stopped at Swiss Chalet for a coffee before going home. I was dreadfully tired and went to bed early. At about 10 p.m., I was awakened by a strong pain deep in my throat. It was very uncomfortable, and so I got up and got a drink of water. The pain eased, and I lay down again. It took only a moment, and the pain came back worse, so I sat up again. I became very nauseated and broke out in a cold sweat.

Feeling very nervous, I sent up a quick prayer asking God to take control, and called my friend Matt. He was just getting ready to go to bed when I said I didn't feel well at all, and thought I should go to the hospital to be checked out. In a few minutes, he came and picked me up. As soon as he told the nurses in emergency that I was having chest pains, they got me right to a bed. They took blood and did an EKG. I was having a heart attack.

I remember feeling panic when the nurses told me, but they calmed me down immediately. The cardiologist that the nurses had called to examine me said that she was going to give me a drug that was a clot buster. They put a needle into my intravenous. The next thing I remember is waking up, and thinking, how weird is that, falling asleep while I am having a heart attack?

It was not until a few days later that I learned that I had gone into severe convulsions because I had an allergic reaction to the drug. The heart attack was pretty mild, but the drug had almost killed me. It was 48 hours before I was off the critical care list in CCU. Five days after my heart attack, the cardiologist did an angiogram. I was still having pain, and he needed to find out why.

The test consisted of a probe being inserted into my heart and flushing my heart with dye so the doctor could see how the blood was flowing through my arteries. I had one artery that was 90 per cent blocked, so it was cleaned out with an inflated balloon connected to the probe, a procedure called an angioplasty. Everything else was functioning as it should, and ten days later after some other tests and treatments, I was released from the hospital.

The doctors would not allow me to go home by myself for a month, so I stayed with my son Stephen and his family in Sarnia. Many prayers had gone up on my behalf, and the most amazing thing to me through all of this was that after the initial panic I experienced, I had such peace and calm. There was a little nervousness now and then, but God's word sustained me. I kept claiming God's promise to me in Isaiah 41:10, "Do not fear, for I am with you; Do not anxiously look about you, for I am your God. I will strengthen you, surely I will help you, Surely I will uphold you with My righteous right hand." His presence with me was very real. He is so faithful. Now when I struggle anew with fear, I remind myself of all He has brought me through. A different trial I faced came a year later.

Earlier I shared the story of my daughter Barbara's Addison's disease. The Lord had answered prayer, and her health had been much better than the doctor's prognosis. This disease had the possibility of an adrenal crisis, when the kidneys fail and death can occur. It is a coma that many never recover from. Barbara's crisis happened on a weekend in June 1996.

Barbara had married and had given birth to a daughter, having no difficulties with either the pregnancy or the birth. I believe this was a miracle from God, because she had been told that she would never have children. She had become ill with what her husband thought was just the flu, but she was much sicker than anyone realized, and after five days of illness, she was raging with fever. On the Friday evening, she was taken into emergency in renal failure.

My son Scott called at about 10 p.m. that Friday night, and said I better come quickly because Barbara was being taken to ICU to be put on life support. It did not look good. Barbara had gone into a coma. The church put her on the prayer chain. I called my friend Marg and asked her if she would drive to Sarnia with me. The family gathered at the hospital with Barbara's husband. Her kidneys had completely shut down and she was filled with septicemia poisoning. The doctors informed all of us that very little hope was held for her recovery. She was 28 years old.

Barbara remained on life support throughout the weekend. I know that many prayers went up to the Lord on her behalf. Her father and I took turns sitting by her bed. None of us left the hospital all weekend. All of a sudden, on Monday, she woke up. Her kidneys were functioning, and the doctors took her off the respirator. By Tuesday afternoon, they were releasing her from the hospital. The young doctor who had admitted her in emergency was a Christian and had called up to ICU several times to see how she was doing. He was the one who told Barbara's dad to tell her that she had received a miracle of healing, because in his words, "nothing we have done has accomplished this." God had answered prayer with a miracle.

As I write this, Barbara has never had another crisis and also has given birth to another child. No understanding is ever given to us of

God's dealings with us, but of one thing I am certain: He loves us and works out His plans for each of us. Those plans are of His design and choosing for our good and His glory. I love to tell this story and trust that each time it is told, He will receive the glory.

The next year brought into my life the deepest valley I have ever walked through. I thought that the loss of my marriage and my home were the darkest days of my life, but ahead of me was something far worse. The death of my oldest son was such a shock and so painful, that I have dreaded to reach this place in this story. To relive the experience of those days is to reawaken the pain and loss, but I know that it must be recorded so that I can share what I learned.

Now that I am retired, every day is Saturday. There are no more mornings of having to get up and go to work. When I was working, how I looked forward to Saturdays. Those were the days I could get up, have a leisurely breakfast, relax, plan my day and not have to watch the time. The old house that I lived in had been made into several apartments. My apartment was on the second floor, and my friend Marg lived on the first. She had a room in the rear with nice windows, and I named it her Florida room. We used to sit and enjoy breakfast there on Saturday mornings with the sun streaming in the window.

That day that turned out to be a day I will never forget started out as just an ordinary mid-summer Saturday. Marg and I had breakfast together, and after I went to my own apartment, I ended up spending an hour on the phone with my daughter-in-law, Elizabeth. When we had time to talk, we loved to just gab about all kinds of things. We talked that Saturday about the Lord, and then got on the topic of family. Of all the things we discussed, we ended up talking about how terrible it would be if something happened to my son Stephen, her husband.

He was out playing touch football with some guys from their church, and it was a very warm and humid morning that Saturday in July of 1997. Elizabeth had warned him to take it easy. The last thing she remembered him saying was, "I will. I will be fine." Apparently he had been complaining about excessive tiredness. He thought he was out of shape and probably needed to lose twenty pounds.

After my phone call, Marg and I decided to go for a walk to a local hardware store. It was close to noon when we left our apartment house. We were walking back from the store when my other son Philip, who lived in London, came racing up the street in his van, pulled over to the curb, jumped out very excitedly and called to us. "Mom, you've got to come home right away; Stephen has been taken to hospital." I remember laughing and saying, "What has he done now, broke his leg or something?" I didn't laugh again for a very long time.

On arriving back at my apartment, I immediately called the hospital in Sarnia. A nurse answered, and I told her who I was, and that I was inquiring about my son. She put Tom on the phone, and when I asked what was wrong with Steve, he just answered me, "You don't want to know."

"What do you mean I don't want to know?" He repeated it.

"You can't mean..." was all I could manage. He said, "Yes. Stephen died."

Stephen was 38 years old. He had a stocky build, and maybe was a little overweight, but he seemed healthy and had no serious illnesses of which anyone was aware. He died of a massive heart attack. I was hysterical. I ran downstairs to Marg's apartment and literally yelled at her, "Stephen's dead! Stephen's dead!" She grabbed me and hugged me.

Then I raced back up the stairs. When I look back at all this, I remember thinking how I had wanted to be calm and quiet in an emergency, but I have an emotional temperament so I reacted emotionally. I remember saying over and over, "Please God, help me!"

Stephen was our oldest son and second child. He was an easy boy to raise because he had a very amiable personality and easy-going temperament. He had his moments, but for the most part, he was a joy. Stephen always loved sports and was patient in explaining them to me. He taught me all about football when he was 16, and I fell in love with the game and still love football to this day. I still miss being able to discuss games with him.

Stephen and Elizabeth had two little girls at the time of his death. Juliann was 8 years old, and Kathryn (called Katie) was 7. Stephen had been saved in 1991 on November 11th. I was in college at the time and still remember his phone call to tell me he had accepted Christ as his personal Savior. I was ecstatic. He went on to really grow in the Lord. He became a Sunday school teacher, and was very involved with Christian sports, especially at the girls' Christian school and at the church. To say that I was devastated by his death is an understatement.

There is no explanation that will suffice when you experience the death of a loved one. Nothing in the immediate eases the shock and pain of your loss. I thank God that His Word that was implanted in me came to my mind to give some comfort. I thought about Romans 8:28, and 1 Corinthians. 10:13. God works all things together for good, and He has promised not to give us more than we can bear. God also comforted me with the words of Psalm 116:15 "Precious in the sight of the Lord Is the death of His godly ones." Once again, as He had done faithfully in the past, God ministered to me from His Word.

Philip, our third oldest son, calmed me down and encouraged me to begin to get things together so we could leave for Sarnia. I knew I had to pack, but I could hardly get my thoughts together. Philip and his wife told me what I needed, and then I realized I would need some clothes for the funeral. I felt frustrated because I could not find the earrings that went with the dress I had chosen. What weird things the mind does! Had it really been only two and a half hours ago that Elizabeth and I were discussing this?

Finally, my suitcase was packed, and we were in Philip's van heading to Sarnia. Philip's wife had just given birth to their first daughter only nine days earlier, so they had to bring along a new baby. I was in the backseat with the baby's car seat. I had not stopped crying since I spoke to Tom on the phone. I prayed and asked the Lord to put a song in my heart so I could get my mind off the reality of what had happened. Hymn after hymn came to my mind, and I sang and hummed all the way to Sarnia.

In the second epistle to the Corinthians, Paul tells us:

> *Blessed be the God and Father of our Lord Jesus Christ, the Father of mercies and God of all comfort; who comforts us in all our affliction so that we will be able to comfort those who are in any affliction with the comfort with which we ourselves are comforted by God. (2 Corinthians 1:3–4)*

Paul calls Him the God of all comfort. Where else can you go when the pain and sorrow are almost unbearable? That is what God did for me that day in the van. He comforted me with the wonderful words of hymns. Many of those songs are Scripture put to music. I will never forget that day when God soothed me with those melodies.

Another lesson that served me well during this time was learning to give thanks in all things, and God gave me an extra measure of grace to be able to thank Him for Stephen's salvation. God had extended His grace to him, and I had peace knowing that he was with Him, done with his old sin nature and all human struggles. Praise God! I had such assurance that Stephen was alive there with Him.

John 14:1–6 is the Scripture read at many funerals. I reminded myself that Jesus had prepared a place for him and had come and taken him home. To this day, I don't spend a lot of time at the cemetery, knowing that Stephen is really not there, only his human remains, but he is alive, at home with Jesus.

Arriving in Sarnia, we found Tom standing outside the emergency department of the hospital. I ran to him, and said, "It's a mistake isn't it? They have made a terrible mistake." He just shook his head and held me. Then we had to go inside, so I could see our son. The whole thing was surreal. I went through the motions, doing and saying what is necessary, but nothing seemed real. Stephen and Elizabeth's girls had been taken to a friend's, but the rest of the family was gathered at the hospital in a separate room. I went in there first and just held Elizabeth. She was almost comatose, not crying, not saying anything, just still in shock. I hugged everyone, as we all cried together. The nurse came to take us to see Stephen.

The paramedics had tried to resuscitate him, but to no avail, so he still had the tube in his mouth. The nurse apologized for that, and explained that an autopsy had to be done to confirm the cause of death, and until that was done the tube could not be removed. He just looked like he was sleeping. I was afraid to touch him, because I didn't want to feel the cold. My memories are a bit foggy, and I can't remember exactly what I said.

Going back out into the hall I found our other son, Michael, sitting in a chair, sobbing uncontrollably. I had never ever seen him cry like that. Michael was two years younger than Stephen, and they had always been close and good friends. He was devastated. We went back to the room with the rest of the family. It was there that I started having chest pains, and a nurse was called for.

Taking me into another room, a cardiac nurse started an intravenous, gave me morphine for the pain and began nitroglycerine. I was having an angina attack. The cardiologist on duty took me to the Cardiac Care Unit, and kept me there overnight. By morning, I was much better. I was released later in the day and went to stay with Elizabeth and the girls.

Much of the next week was a blur, and only a few things stand out in my mind. Facing the funeral was the first difficult task at hand. I don't even remember being at the funeral home in the afternoon, but in the evening when we arrived for the visitation time, I was amazed at all the cars. We could hardly find a parking space there were so many cars, and I remember a line of people halfway round the building. I was with Tom, Elizabeth and the girls, and said, "Look at all the people; someone important must have died." I was thinking of a politician, or someone very well-known in the community. I had no idea all these people were there because of Stephen.

We had arrived about 6:40 p.m., and the visitation line continued until one of the staff finally locked the door at 10:30 p.m. There had been over 600 people through for visitation. The funeral service had to be moved to the church because so many people were expected and over 800 people came. What a joy for me to realize how many people were influenced and touched by my son's life.

One of the hardest moments I experienced, was when the time came to leave our son at the cemetery. Only a parent can imagine the agony of leaving her child alone there and walking away. It was my faith that made it possible that day, by believing that Stephen was with the Lord. All during the visitation and funeral, I was able to see his human remains, but there came the time when I knew I would never see him again in this life. This has been the hardest part of my story to write because I relive the emotions as the memories resurface. Stephen's legacy encourages me to do this.

Because Stephen was so involved with sports, and particularly an avid golfer, his golf club named a tournament after him which takes place once a year, and the girl's Christian school gives a sports award named for him every year at graduation. Stephen had also been a hockey referee since he was fourteen, and now there is a hockey league named in his honour.

Another episode that moved me was a few moments with Tom. At the time of Stephen's death, we had been apart seventeen years and saw very little of each other. Our paths would cross at family events, but outside of those, we had no contact. I had forgotten that when Stephen, our first son was born, Tom had given me a dozen beautiful red roses. At the funeral home among all the floral arrangements sat a vase with a dozen red roses marked, "To Steve, love Dad."

After the funeral luncheon, when almost everyone had gone, Tom came to me and gave me the roses. He simply said, "I gave you a dozen roses when Steve was born, now I will give you these dozen roses I bought for him." I was so emotionally overwhelmed, all I could do was cling to him and cry. I have kept the vase and put it away.

It was few days later at Elizabeth's, when I first heard the whole story of what had happened to Stephen. Apparently the heat and humidity that Saturday was really bothering him, and while playing touch foot-ball, he began to feel ill. He left the game saying he wasn't feeling well, and went and sat down under a tree. Several men from the church were there, and two of them were actually doctors. No one seemed aware of how seriously ill he was.

He found no relief under the tree and decided to go home. He had only gone about two blocks, when he slumped over the wheel of his van. A car coming toward him was bumped by him, but another driver saw him slumped over the wheel, and directed his car into his path to stop Stephen's vehicle. Someone called 911. The paramedics did everything they could to resuscitate him, but he was already gone. The doctor that did the autopsy told Elizabeth that even if it had happened at the hospital, the attack was so severe they would not have been able to save him.

When God determines the time to go home, that's what will happen. We do not receive an explanation. All of us mortals must put on immortality (1 Corinthians 15:53). We know we cannot go into eternity as we are.

Psalm 139:16 says that God has written down in His book "all" the days that are ordained for us. That writing includes our birthday and our death day. Isaiah writes in Chapter 55 that God is so infinite, that His working has not been given to us to understand. Again we see the same Biblical principal in the familiar Proverbs. 3:5-7. Do not try to figure out what God is doing, but place every area of your life in His hand and trust Him to work out His plan. The old hymn, "Trust and Obey", puts it in a nutshell: "Trust and Obey, for there's no other way, to be happy in Jesus, you must trust and obey." We are to put our faith in Him in every area of our lives and leave the results with Him.

All of God's purposes for Stephen's death at a young age may never be known, but there were a few very dramatic results. A few men of his age who were not walking with the Lord rededicated their lives, and one young woman's husband was saved. The most dramatic thing of all that happened was that Stephen's dad came to the Lord.

During the first week after the funeral, Tom came to Elizabeth's every day. He just wanted to be with family where he could talk about Stephen. Both Elizabeth and I talked a lot about Stephen being with the Lord, and how that gave us comfort and peace. Tom was very agitated by that, and indignantly asked how we could possibly know that. We shared many Scripture verses with him that taught about God's promises to those who had received Christ. By God's grace, we were able to show him joy over the assurance we had in these truths.

Tom shared that he had been very pleased and touched by the funeral service and was very impressed with the pastor who had conducted it. At the wake, the pastor had told Tom to call him, and they could go for a coffee and talk. Two weeks after the funeral he did that.

The pastor took him for coffee, and then they went back to the church office and just talked. It was there that the pastor presented the Gospel to Tom, and assured him that he could see Stephen again. Tom got down on his knees, and with many tears prayed and asked Jesus to save him. Praise God! Luke 15:7 tells us, "There will be more joy in heaven over one sinner who repents." Stephen's death had brought about more repentance than just one sinner. I know that if God had given Stephen the choice, he would have gladly given up his life, if it meant his father's salvation. Stephen had prayed for his dad all the time.

The salvation of a soul is worth more than anything to God. We can see that truth played out in the enormous cost of Calvary. Father and Son both paid a price that cannot be estimated. "He made Him who knew no sin to be sin on our behalf, so that we might become the righteousness of God in Him" (2 Corinthians 5:21). Let your mind drink this in. God let His Holy, beloved Son become Sin. Jesus became filth in the Father's eyes for us. God had to turn away. Feel the pain they both endured when you read in Matthew 27:46, "MY GOD, MY GOD, WHY HAVE YOU FORKSAKEN ME?" This is the first and last time in all of eternity that they would be separated. That is the cost of our salvation.

These truths have made Stephen's death much easier to bear because God caused me to understand that He too knows the pain of being separated from His beloved Son. They were reunited soon after, and my comfort is that I too will see my son again one day.

Most people will tell you that when you are going through this process of burying a loved one, it is like being in a fog. You go through the hours and the days, without awareness of things. I really believe that the Lord carried me through. I am convinced of this because of my daughter-in-law. Elizabeth and I have remained very close, and she still insists that she would not have made it through the whole ordeal if it were not for me

Elizabeth's whole family was there. She is one of seven children, three girls and four boys. Her mom and dad came to the house immediately on learning of Stephen's death. I was so burdened for Elizabeth and the girls, wondering how they would manage to get through all this.

Many people were coming and going, and I knew that there was food to be prepared and coffee to serve. I had stayed with Stephen and Elizabeth's many times, and knew the house very well, so I helped manage these things. Elizabeth's mother, although a delightful woman, was not a hostess and was at a loss in that position. The busyness also made it easier for me because it gave me less time to think of myself and how I was feeling. I stayed there for two weeks, looking after their needs. Elizabeth has always told me that she will never forget that even though I had just lost my son, I stepped in to take care of them.

Our oldest daughter Nancy and her husband had come alongside Elizabeth to take care of the funeral arrangements and all the other financial needs. Because Stephen had died in his car, it was only natural that Elizabeth wanted a different vehicle and they helped her arrange to get a new car.

Paul admonishes us in Philippians 2:4 "do not merely look out for your own personal interests, but also for the interests of others." It was the supernatural work of God in our situation, that by concentrating on helping Elizabeth and the girls, I was blessed because my mind was focused on them and not on my own grief. I would have enough time down the road to grieve.

It has been such a blessing to me that I had been with Stephen and his family many times in the last year of his life. He was a good son. He was not a perfect man. His wife could probably tell you stories, but we won't go there. Stephen and I had a good relationship. Two days before his death, he was in London at my home. We had a good visit, and I hugged him, told him I loved him, and said good-bye, not realizing I was really saying good-bye. I wanted to record this, so you could understand that I have great peace and joy, knowing that there was no unfinished business between us. I will always be thankful for that.

Experiencing the death of a loved one is one thing, working your way through grief is much different. During my college classes on counseling, I had studied a great deal about grief and grief counseling. I had even had opportunity to do grief counseling in the jails. I had learned all about the stages of grief, and even had counseled people how to work through them. But learning about it from a book, and living it out are like night and day. If I had thought much about it I would have told myself, "Hang on, it is going to be a bumpy ride."

Returning to work after a trauma apparently is very therapeutic for some people, because busyness can be an antidote for grief. Unfortunately, that did not help me, so I didn't go back to work for about six weeks. I had a harder time controlling my emotions after I came home from Sarnia than I did in the first two weeks. When I did finally return to work, I had several instances where I got angry with a fellow worker and had to apologize. Work was difficult, and so, in 1999 when there was a downsizing at the Salvation Army, and because of my age, I took an early retirement.

Grief unsettles you. This was my experience after Stephen's death. I had lived in my apartment for nine years, and loved it, and then I ended up moving five times in the next five years. I also struggled with health issues and had angina attacks occur occasionally. At that time, I didn't realize how my grief was affecting me. It's much easier to see what is going on in other peoples' lives than it is in your own.

During those five years, I persevered in walking with the Lord. I was still doing jail ministry, teaching Bible studies, and teaching a Sunday school class. It was a time when I held on to the Lord and my faith with everything I had. My foundation had been built on the solid rock, and so I did not crumble. Sometimes I struggled to stand, but never completely fell. Psalm 37:23–24 tells us, "The steps of a man are established by the Lord, And He delights in his way. When he falls, he shall not be hurled headlong, Because the Lord is the One who holds his hand." Take notice it says "when" he falls, not "if" he falls. We all will have experiences that cause us to stumble, but we can be assured, that He is there holding us up.

John 11:35 is the shortest verse in the Bible, and a very familiar one. Two little words are recorded to express how Jesus felt at the death of Lazarus: "Jesus wept." In those two little words are a range of emotions that is comparable to riding a roller coaster. Coater riding means you are thrown up and down, your stomach gets unsettled, and you just want to get you feet back on solid ground. That is what grief was like for me.

The other description of grief is that it is like waves that come and wash over you, and knock you off your feet. I would have some good days, then a bad one. Time is a great healer, and as time passes, grief lessens. There is one thing I will never understand, and that is how people get through these things without the Lord.

Now that I was retired, there wasn't a firm reason to stay in London. In 2002, an opportunity came for me to move back to Sarnia, and with both my daughters living there, and many of my grandchildren, I moved back to what I thought of as home.

I had lived in London for fourteen years. When I moved to London in 1988, I had no idea what the next fourteen years would bring. I had the incredible privilege of studying the Word of God, and knowing the Word helped me put it into practice, through many difficulties.

From the joys I had in studying and jail ministry, to the darkest valley that I have ever walked through, God has made Himself real to me. I remember in the early days with Lois, that she had taught me to pray, "Lord make my security in you real to me." He answered my prayer. Now I was going home. Whatever paths might lie ahead of me I didn't know, but I did know I would not walk them alone.

I would like to close this chapter by sharing a precious thing that God did for me. It was in the first year after Stephen's death. I was still having days when I could hardly get it together.

One particular Sunday, I was not able to stop crying. By early afternoon, I felt exhausted, and was lying down on my bed. I just lay there pouring out my aching heart to the Lord. "Lord, if only I could have one more visit with Stephen. I just want to see him again for a few moments." I fell sound asleep and had the most wonderful dream about my son. We were together talking and laughing, and it was so real, that when I woke up later, I was smiling and felt such peace. All my heartache of earlier was gone, and I remembered every detail. I was praising the Lord, thanking Him, rejoicing over the time with my son.

The Apostle Paul uses the word "confidence" in many of his writings. He wanted his readers to know that they could put their complete confidence in God. We can too. He loves us with an unconditional, everlasting love that does not depend on our performance level. He is a compassionate God who comforts us in all our sorrow, and He is faithful and dependable. I trust that in sharing my experience, you will be encouraged to have confidence in Him.

FOURTEEN
Home

When you hear the word "home," what image comes to your mind? I am a homebody, so for me, this word conjures up images of coziness. I see a comfortable chair, a blanket, and something warm and comforting to drink. Will you have tea, coffee, or hot chocolate, anyone?

When my family was young, the place to be was in the kitchen. The smells and sounds came from steaming pots on the stove, something baking in the oven and many voices all raised in chatter. I think of hot stew and warm homemade bread for dinner; what is more comforting than that?

The Christmas season in particular, brings nostalgia for me as the time for decorating or baking comes around. The memories flood back and I miss our house. I decorated every nook and cranny and baked up a storm in the large kitchen that had loads of cupboard and counter space. In my memories, that house says home.

Homesickness was a struggle for me when I was young, and it has followed me into adulthood. I still like to be in my own bed each night. I go away from time to time, but can't wait to get "home." Even through the years of a difficult marriage, I still preferred home to anywhere else. Tom, Nancy and I moved from St. Thomas, Ontario to Sarnia in 1957, and though I had been gone from this place for a number of years, I was glad to be coming home.

Barbara had rented a small house and signed a year's lease. She was gone most of the summer of 2002, so in July, I came to Sarnia and stayed in her house. My apartment in London had no air conditioning, and that adorable little house had central air. It was not difficult to decide to spend my summer there.

The top priority that summer was to find a church family. The church I had always attended when I had lived in Sarnia previously had built a larger building, and now the morning service was attended by nearly a thousand people. They had also expanded their music program, and I found it extremely loud. I'm sure the Lord enjoys it, but my ears do not. In developing a hearing loss, I found that I could not handle the loud music. I had always gone to a smaller church, and that is what I was comfortable with, so the realization came that I had to find a new church home. I needed the Lord's guidance, so I prayed that He would lead me to where He wanted me to fellowship and serve.

Elizabeth and the girls had also moved away from Sarnia for a couple of years, and when they decided to move back, I went to help them. Their next door neighbor came to see if she could help, and in our conversation she shared that they attended a small church just outside of Sarnia. She invited me to come with them the following Sunday, so the arrangements were made for me to go. From that first Sunday in People's Church, I felt at home.

Barbara did not come back to the house to live, and because the owner knew me, he allowed me to take over her lease, so my summer stay in Sarnia became a permanent move. I gave up my London apartment, and by the end of October was settled in the house with my own belongings. The sense of coming home increased.

Living in Sarnia and going to People's seemed like the perfect fit. For a year, I attended everything at the church. I went to the Ladies Bible Study group, the Ministry of Women meetings, and the senior's group called the "Sonshiners." I wanted to get to know the people and wanted them to know me. I wanted to be involved.

In the spring, I made arrangements to go to the annual ladies retreat. It was there that I met Myrna. We spent a great deal of time talking, and it soon seemed like we had known each other forever. She became very special to me.

Myrna had taken on the responsibility of leading the Ministry of Women and wanted to start a special ministry at the church. She had a burden on her heart for the younger moms at People's. As a young mom with two boys, Myrna had attended a Bible study group designed just for the moms of pre-school children. She attended with the same ladies for five years. It was her desire that we could begin something with the same design. She had been praying that the Lord would bring someone to teach this program. After talking for a few hours, she asked if I would be willing to do the teaching.

Believing that God has given me a gift of exhortation and teaching has led me to do a number of speaking engagements at Women's Ministry meetings around our county as the opportunity presented itself, and I had been teaching Bible studies consistently since my time spent with Lois. I was excited that Myrna had asked me and sensed the Lord opening a door to a new ministry. I responded in the usual way and promised her I would go home and seek the Lord's will in prayer. I must confess that I said yes with much trepidation. I knew that I was not adequate for the job at hand, but had learned that I am a vessel "chosen of God, holy and beloved" (Colossians 3:12) whom He has chosen to use, and that He is quite adequate for the job.

Myrna and I prayed much and drew up a plan that she presented to the elder's board. It was approved. Our next step was to pray about the material, and what the Lord would have me teach. As I shared with Myrna the discipleship lessons that I had been given by Lois, we felt comfortable about that being the place to start. By September, we were ready. For the beginning session, I offered my home.

The first Tuesday morning, Myrna came prepared to do the child-care while I was teaching. I can still hear myself saying, "Myrna, I am so new at the church, no one really knows me. I don't think anyone will come." She just smiled and replied, "Wait and see." First one mom, and then another drove up. Five moms in all came. I am ashamed to admit I was amazed. By this time I should have learned that God can accomplish what He desires. That was the simple beginning of four exciting years. God had again moved me into uncharted territory.

The longing of my heart is to share everything God did in those four years, but I know I must encapsulate them for you. That first year we continued into the spring, and ended the middle of May; I used all my own material. The second year we studied a parenting book, *Parenting With Purpose & Grace,* by Alice Fryling. The next year we did a study of Proverbs 31, *Beautiful in God's Eyes,* by Elizabeth George, and the last year we went through Johanna Weaver's books, *Having a Mary Heart in a Martha World*, and *Having a Mary Spirit.*

Our plans also included social times. Another woman named Karen had come into the group to help with the organization of events. There was an assortment of activities, including gathering at a park a few times during the summers, barbeques, going out to lunch as a group, and potlucks at the church. We organized Christmas events, and we put together evening socials that would include the husbands. We used volunteer workers for our nursery, and for some of the socials, those volunteers would stay after Bible study and care for the children while the moms had time together. I was blessed over and over.

Myrna's vision came to life. The mom's group started with five and by the third year, there were thirty. Word had spread, and our moms had begun inviting ladies from other churches. The fourth year the attendance was less because some of the ladies were starting to home school. I would see them on Sunday mornings, and they would tell me how much they missed coming. I was moved to offer evening studies in my home, and so I would repeat the morning study in the evening.

Titus 2:3 is specific with instructions for the older women, and I don't see it as optional. As the opportunity comes, we are to fulfill this command. In remembering Lois, I used to say to the Lord, "Just give me a younger woman who will listen to me, and I will gladly teach them." God did "far more abundantly beyond all that we ask or think, according to the power that works within us" (Ephesians 3:20).

God melded our group together, and it turned into four incomparable years. I received many cards, notes, and gifts from the moms, and was awed by the fact that I received notes and cards from the husbands. At the end of the third year, after finishing Proverbs 31, an anonymous note came to me from one of the husbands that said there had been such a change in his wife that their home was a different place. Praise God!

Every time you teach, you as the teacher are confronted by the Word of God. Over the years of the mom's study I continued to learn and grow. Week by week, the lessons spoke to the moms, and in this process

God was also speaking to my heart, working through my study and preparation, to make me more like His Son.

In addition to the Bible study, a mentoring ministry started. As I shared my experiences, how God used the time with Lois to give me a firm foundation, and ground me in the Word, some of the moms asked if I would consider mentoring. It flourished also.

Of all the books we studied, I enjoyed Johanna Weaver's "*Mary Books*" the most. She is a well-read author, and shared many things she learned from other books. She gives some wonderful illustrations. Especially two have stayed with me.

The first illustration concerns carrying burdens that God never gave you. The story is of a man walking up a mountainside pulling a wagon. The Lord stops him and asks him to take some rocks to the top of the mountain for Him. The man agrees with joy. He is going along singing, when on his trip several people ask him to take rocks for them also.

Soon he stops singing, and starts complaining of the heavy burden in his wagon. "Why has the Lord given me such a heavy burden? I can't do this," he grumbles. Past the halfway point up the mountain, he again meets the Lord. "What is the matter?" the Lord asks him. "The load you have given me is too heavy!" cries the man.

The Lord looks in the wagon, and begins throwing out rocks. "I never gave you this load," says the Lord. When the wagon was emptied of all the extra rocks, the man's joy returned, and he went on his way singing. Examine your load, and see what you are carrying. Do you have burdens that God never intended you to carry?

The week we did this lesson, I received a phone call asking me to teach another study. We don't like to admit that we are motivated by pride in these situations, but I felt good about being asked. I said yes. Then this lesson came up, and it was clear to me I had let someone else put a rock in my wagon. I had the mom's study, the evening study, and mentoring going on; another study would have put me in overload. Praise God, I asked forgiveness for my pride, called them back, and said I was sorry, but I was unable to do what they asked.

No matter whom we are, teacher or student, we must always be on guard against whatever way Satan would rob us of being where God wants us. He never gives us more than we can handle, but sometimes we do it to ourselves.

The second illustration from Weaver that sticks in my mind was a demonstration on priorities. A time management professor was trying to make a point in class. He produced a glass jar, and put rocks in it to the top. He asked the class "is the jar full?" Some said "yes." The professor then added some gravel to the jar, then some sand, and finally water. With each addition he asked the same question. Most of the students replied, "Probably not." Then he asked, "What is this lesson about?" No one answered. "You must put the big rocks in the jar first," he told them.

Jesus gives us the same message in Matthew 6:33, "But seek first His kingdom and His righteousness, and all these things will be added to you." Keep your priorities straight. Do you rush into your day without a quiet time with the Lord and His Word? How much time do you spend in prayer seeking His wisdom and guidance concerning your activities, finances, and service? I can still hear Lois' voice saying to me, "if you are too busy for God, you are too busy." From time to time the Lord has to remind me to put my big rocks in the jar first.

Many changes took place in me over those years teaching the mom's Bible study. The Lord, through His Word and the power of the Holy

Spirit, gave me victory over many of my sin habits. Two things that the Lord especially convicted me of were that I wasted too much time reading secular fiction, and watching television. I have now reduced the time I spend reading secular fiction, and have also redesigned my TV watching. God truly makes a way of escape when we really want to see it (1 Corinthians 10:13).

A few weeks ago I was visiting with my son, Scott, and said, "Would you have ever thought that one day I would be teaching young women how to be Godly wives, mothers, and homemakers?" He just looked at me and said "No."

The start of this book does not go back to when my children were very young. I have not recorded any details of that time, only a glimpse. I was not a Christian, and I was an angry, impatient young mom. I was an, "I command, you obey mom", and I can tell you I did not like her. There is a road of regrets behind me, but praise God, He has renewed my mind so much that the mom my children remember from their childhood does not exist today. In her place, lives a woman with Biblical perspectives toward the mom's role. God has made something beautiful out of my life and given it eternal value. I am, of all women, most blessed.

During the Bible study years, I had also come alongside Myrna and served with the Ministry of Women. We developed such a love for one another and had close times of fellowship and prayer. After Bible study on a Tuesday, she would grab some KFC, and we would have lunch, make plans, and pray for all the ladies ministries.

It was a terrible shock, when in October of 2006, at 57 years of age, Myrna was killed in a car accident one Sunday morning on her way to Sunday school. Isaiah 55 came to my mind again, reminding me that we cannot always understand His ways. I will miss her for a long time, but it is comforting to know I will see her in glory.

The fourth year of the mom's study was a difficult one because I developed some physical problems. By spring, I knew that I could not make a commitment to teach another year as I was facing surgery. I knew that there would be no value in my teaching if it was not the Lord's will, so I stepped away from the study, and the new Ministry of Women leader took over.

The study thrived without me, but I must confess that at the time I struggled with a sense of loss. I knew my time with the moms was over. What would be awaiting me around the corner in this walk with the Lord? My mind could never conceive what the Lord's plans were.

FIFTEEN
A Grain of Sand

Living on the Great Lakes means for most people that some time is spent at the beach. Personally I love it, but the pesky grains of sand get between my toes, and if the wind blows, it gets in my hair and eyes. When I come home to unload the car there is sand every where. It's in the backseat, the trunk, the clothes, the towels, and the worst part is, it gets tracked into the house. I remember the children would fight to be the first one in the shower, because they felt so gritty.

Have you ever stooped to try to pick up one grain of sand? A grain of sand is so tiny it is virtually impossible to pick up. In the Old Testament it is recorded that the sands of the seas cannot be measured, nor the descendants of King David (Jeremiah 33:22). In the New Testament, Paul uses the same illustration quoting the prophet Isaiah, "THOUGH THE NUMBER OF THE SONS OF ISRAEL BE LIKE THE SAND OF THE SEA" (Romans 9:27). The Scripture here again gives us a simple human picture to depict a spiritual truth, and we need to see that just as the sand cannot be measured, neither can the number of the children of God be counted. We are included in that number.

In God's whole eternal scheme of things, we are as a grain of sand. How could one grain of sand bring glory to the eternal almighty

God? Only our God knows. As I walk step by step along the way, I have learned that I know very little. The more I learned about my Heavenly Father, the more the insufficiency of my knowledge became apparent to me, and so my daily prayer became "fit me into your plan." He is the only one that knows our today's from our tomorrows. I am again reminded of Psalm 139:16, "Your eyes have seen my unformed substance; And in Your book were all written The days that were ordained for me, When as yet there was not one of them." and also Jeremiah 29:11, "'For I know the plans that I have for you,' declares the Lord, 'plans for welfare and not for calamity to give you a future and a hope.'"

God will lead us down paths that are strange to us, but not to Him. We must get to know Him and His Word, so that our confidence is in Him and not in ourselves. Then we can step out in faith, being assured that He is leading on the path that is right for each of us, and then we need not be afraid because the path is a strange one. In Acts 16:6–9 we read that the Holy Spirit blocked Paul from going to Bithynia, and then gave him a vision to go to Macedonia. He directed Paul to the place He wanted him to be, so that he could be used according to God's plan. At the time, Paul may not have understood why his way was blocked. God will also direct our ways when we learn to trust Him in every area of our lives. It is the familiar promise from Proverbs. 3:6, "In all your ways acknowledge Him, And He will make your paths straight."

In an earlier chapter, I mentioned about the way the Scripture tells us how God intervenes in lives and situations with "But God". Even though I was on a waiting list for surgery, I was asked to continue my evening Bible study, and I agreed. I believed God would meet my needs for two hours once a week. It was during that study that the idea for this book surfaced. Prov. 16:9 tells us how God intervenes: "The mind of man plans his way, But the Lord directs his steps." How absurd to think that I could write a book. But God said, Psalm 37:4 "Delight yourself in the Lord; And He will give you the desires of your heart." What are the desires of my heart? Ever since I went to a mission's conference in 1988, my desire has been that my life would bring glory to God.

God used that mission's conference to direct my steps to new paths. I left my home, and my family, went to college, worked in a hostel with homeless men, visited jail, traveled the highways, and then came full circle home to teach young moms. I have had some mountaintop experiences, and walked through some deep dark valleys. I have come to this place where the outer person, though older, looks reasonably the same, but inside, there has been a miraculous change. I have traveled from a place of utter despair, to delighting myself in Him.

Psalm 139 gives us a clear portrait of how intimately God knows us. He is omniscient and omnipresent in our lives. He is the creator and created each of us as a unique individual. Verse 13 says, "For You formed my inward parts; You wove me in my mother's womb." Verses 17–18 go on to tell us that we are in God's thoughts. "How precious also are Your thoughts to me, O God! How vast is the sum of them! If I should count them, they would outnumber the sand. When I awake, I am still with You." He delights in His creation. All of His creation was created for His pleasure and that includes us (Revelation 4:11). One thing I do believe is that He wants us to learn to "delight ourselves in Him," as He delights in us.

As I come to the end of my writing, I do know I am facing surgery, and although I do not know what my tomorrows hold, I am confident that God has me safe in His hand. So I am standing at a new corner once again, ready to walk around it, trusting God that whatever direction this path leads me, He is sufficient to accomplish His will. My 69th birthday is coming quickly, and be assured that whatever age you are right now, whether young or old, you are still an instrument that God can use. I have written this book in the faith that God will receive the glory from the record of my walk with Him, as I rose from a place of despair to a place of delight.

AFTERWORD

Three months have passed since I finished the last chapter of *From Despair to Delight* at the end of January 2008. At that time I did not know what God wanted to do with my written story. I thought that His purpose for me could just be a personal discipline process, as I had found it so hard to sit down and write. I believed with all my heart that He wanted me to do this, and yet had no idea that God might want my manuscript published.

The day I finished typing the last word on the last page I simply bowed my head and said, "Here is your book Lord. I give this to you to do what you want with it. Lord if you want it published, you will have to intervene as I do not know one thing about how to get a book published." With that prayer I got up and walked away from the computer.

It was only four or five days later when walking down the hall in my building I noticed a stack of papers laying on the bench near the main door. Out of curiosity I picked one off the pile. The title across the top of the front page read, "This Week in Sarnia," so I thought I would take one home to read. It consisted of only a few pages, but the article on the third page caught my eye.

The article was approximately half the page and was a story of someone I knew. It was about a fellow named John who had written a book. I was intrigued, because I have known John for a number of years. During the eighties I was involved with the young peoples and college and career departments at Temple Baptist Church. John had attended there and was a friend of my daughter Barbara's. The article told John's story of writing a book and having it published, and also that he had another to come out at a later date.

Was God opening a door, I wondered? I called John and left a message telling him about my story, and asking him if I could pick his brain about publishing. The next day, he called me back, and we talked for quite a while. He told me all about getting his book published through Morgan James Publishing, and then John gave me David Hancock's email address, (founder of Morgan James).

I sent off an email to David Hancock telling him about my book, and received an answer about three hours later. He said it sounded wonderful and one of his staff would be in touch. I received a phone call February 6, from David Sauer, Senior Author Liaison Executive for Morgan James Publishing. We chatted for a while and I told him all about myself and my story. He told me he would email me with an email address for the Morgan James drop box, so I could send my manuscript to them to see if it would be accepted for publication.

It was Friday, February 8, 2008 when I emailed the manuscript. On Thursday, February the 14th, I received an email back from David Sauer. I could hardly bring myself to open it. Finally, after a few moments I talked myself into opening it to see what the answer was. With the butterflies in my stomach totally out of control, I clicked on it, and there written in capital letters was the message, "CONGRATULATIONS. Your manuscript has been accepted." I was ecstatic! It was one of the best Valentine gifts I had ever received. It had been only a little over two weeks since I finished writing my story and it already had been accepted for publication. Another miracle had happened in my life.

As each need has arisen in this process of bringing my manuscript to publication, there has been someone in my life who has come forward to meet that need. Ephesians 2:10 says "For we are His workmanship, created in Christ Jesus for good works, which God prepared beforehand so that we would walk in them." God had details arranged before He ever led me to sit down at the computer. For instance, my editor Beth Ann was my prayer partner for two years before I ever needed her as an editor. Last year, I did not realize her Master's Degree was in Education. I was praying for her as she worked to get her degree, but I did not realize then what that would mean to me. Beth Ann was not only qualified to do the job, but came with a willing spirit to do it. The hours that she has put in are too numerous to count. I trust that God will bless her richly for her contribution in this process. I also needed someone very knowledgeable in computers, and thank God for my son Scott, who has the knowledge and has endlessly helped me with the computer.

Scott's gift to me for Christmas 2005 was a new computer. He didn't just go out and buy me one, he built it himself. Then, in late 2006, he upgraded it for me. I want to believe that the Lord gave him all these great ideas so that when the time came for me to write, I would have a good computer to do it on. Certainly Scott had no idea at the time what a really great thing he was doing for me. He has done so many things for me with the computer, for which I am so thankful, and also showed me how to do things I had trouble with. God's provision, however it comes into our lives, is always sufficient.

One Sunday morning, after the morning worship service was over, Rose came into the foyer, and sat down beside me. We started chatting, I told her about writing my story, and that it was being published. She asked me about the cover. I just told her at that point I was not sure about it. She is an artist, who does sketches, and paints in oils and watercolors. I had no idea about her talent. She willingly offered her remarkable gift to this project to help design the cover. Again I could see that God already had someone prepared with the ability to do what I could not do. Truthfully, I cannot draw a straight line without a ruler. Rose has made a great contribution to this book.

So now I, and everyone who has had a part in this publication, must leave the results in the Lord's hands. I know He has a purpose, and He is able to guide and direct to fulfill it. I trust that this story will be a blessing and encouragement to all who read it.

REFERENCES

"Scripture taken from the NEW AMERICAN STANDARD BIBLE, Copyright 1960, 1962, 1963, 1968, 1971, 1972, 1973, 1975, 1977, 1995 by The Lockman Foundation. Used by permission. www.Lockman.org"

Parenting with Purpose & Grace. Copyright 2006 by Alice Fryling. WaterbrookPress, Colorado Springs, CO. All rights reserved.

Reprinted from *Having a Mary Heart in a Martha World*. Copyright 2000, 2002, 2007 by Joanna Weaver. Waterbrook Press, Colorado Springs, CO. All rights reserved.

Reprinted from *Having a Mary Spirit*. Copyright 2006 by Joanna Weaver. Waterbrook Press, Colorado Springs, CO. All rights reserved.

The Power of His Presence: A Year of Devotions from the Writings of Ray Stedman / Ray C. Stedman; compiled by Mark Mitchell. Copyright 2006 by Elaine Stedman. Discovery House Publishers, Grand Rapids, Michigan.

Webster's Ninth New Collegiate Dictionary. Copyright 1987 by Merriam-Webster Inc. Thomas Allen & Son Limited, Markham, Ontario.

ABOUT THE AUTHOR

Patricia Freeman has lived all of her life in Southwestern, Ontario, Canada, and has lived in Sarnia, Ontario since 1957. She is the divorced mother of six, and grandmother of fourteen, and step-grandmother to three. After twenty-five years of homemaking, she moved to London, Ontario and started a new career as a Christian Addictions Counselor. She focused on alcoholism, drug addiction, gambling, and also grief counseling. Employed by the Salvation Army in London, Ontario, working with transients, and prison inmates, she has travelled throughout the Province of Ontario, visiting in most of the prisons and jails. Her jail ministry spanned eleven years.

After her eldest son's death in 1997, she took an early retirement from her position with the Salvation Army, but continued to visit in the prisons and jails for a few more years, and continued to counsel on a volunteer basis. She moved back to Sarnia in 2002, where she now lives near her children and grandchildren. This first time author is presently involved with speaking to women's groups on occasion, is a one-on-one counselor and mentor, and a Bible Study teacher.